F X Velarde

F X Velarde

Dominic Wilkinson
and Andrew Crompton

The Twentieth Century Society

Published by Liverpool University Press on behalf of
Historic England, The Engine House, Fire Fly Avenue, Swindon SN2 2EH
www.HistoricEngland.org.uk

Historic England is a Government service championing England's heritage and giving expert,
constructive advice.

The views expressed in this book are those of the authors and not necessarily those of
Historic England.

First published 2020
ISBN 978-1-78962-814-2 paperback

British Library Cataloguing in Publication data
A CIP catalogue record for this book is available from the British Library.

Series editors: Timothy Brittain-Catlin, Barnabas Calder, Elain Harwood and Alan Powers

Page layout by Carnegie Book Production
Printed in the Czech Republic via Akcent Media Limited.

Front cover: RC Shrine of Our Lady of Lourdes, Blackpool; detail of column
Frontispiece: Choir gallery, English Martyrs RC church, Wallasey
Back cover: Velarde in his Gordon England 'Cup' Austin 7, France 1928

Contents

Foreword

Architecture underwent a great change in the first half of the twentieth century, spanning the world wars, and my father was one of its innovators. This book investigates both his influences and his evolution.

My own career was heavily influenced by observing and in a small way sharing his work, and I had always been destined to follow in my father's footsteps; however, I was dyslexic as a child, which was a real handicap. I think he was aware of this, as he had been called 'a mutt' in his youth and may have had the same problem. Consequently he was completely supportive of me in all the career decisions I made to follow the path of design rather than architecture.

One of my earliest recollections of my father's working life was going with him to visit the sculptor Herbert Tyson Smith in his studio in Liverpool's Bluecoat Chambers. He was never without a raw onion, which he ate like an apple, and the scent of this mixed with my father's Abdullah cigarettes conjures up many happy memories.

In my teens I made models for my father out of cartridge paper, and drew visuals to clarify his ideas to clients. He preferred always to build in brick because he was taught in brick, which was the norm just after the First World War. It should be remembered that this was ten years before the advent of Le Corbusier and concrete.

He designed everything inside his churches and the fact that he was only five foot four probably accounted for all the pews and seats in his churches being on the small side. As a family we found it very funny when he came walking home from the station, since all we could see was a bowler hat bobbing along the top of the hedge.

Frank, as he was known, was not a rich man, although he made a comfortable living. He always dressed beautifully in tailor-made suits, and was very fond of gold and silver possessions such as pens and cufflinks. Some of his colleagues at Liverpool University were also interested in antiques and one of them pointed him towards a shop in Chester. He had seen, and paid for, a silver snuff box which he went to collect later. The salesperson told him that 'the lady over there' wanted the snuff box and insisted

English Martyrs RC church, view from St Georges Road

on having it; but he informed the haughty woman sharply that it was his, and refused to give it up. He later discovered that it was Queen Mary, who was in the habit of nearly always getting her own way.

I am so proud that my father is now beginning to get the recognition he deserves. For this I am grateful to historian Dr Elain Harwood for getting the ball rolling; to Dr Andrew Crompton at the School of the Arts, Liverpool School of Architecture and Dominic Wilkinson of LJMU School of Art and Design. They have visited me at home more than once, and it has been an enormous pleasure to talk with them about my Dad.

Giles Velarde
August 2020

Acknowledgements

This book would not have been possible without the generosity of time and spirit offered by Giles and Celia Velarde. Their insight into F X Velarde the man, and support with identifying the limited remaining archival material has been invaluable.

The series editor Elain Harwood has gone beyond the description this title implies and special thanks are due for her patience and diligence.

The assistance of the following people and organisations has also been invaluable: Neil Sayer at the Archdiocese of Liverpool Archives, Robyn Orr and Eleanor McKenzie at Liverpool University Special Collections and Archives, Father Peter Phillips at the Diocese of Shrewsbury Archives, Sue Poole for her work on Herbert Tyson Smith, Professor John Tarn for his encouragement, the Paul Mellon Foundation for supporting the early research with a travel grant and Liverpool John Moores University and the University of Liverpool for assistance with publication.

For the many photographs of the surviving churches we are indebted to Alun Bull, Steven Baker, Chris Redgrave and James O Davies at Historic England; for the new line drawings Matthew Usher and Isaac Crompton; and the RIBA and National Trust for the images from their collections. We are grateful to our editors at Liverpool University Press and Sarah Enticknap formerly of Historic England.

We would also like to thank Maria West and SPEC at The Grail, the priests in charge and their churchwardens for generously allowing access to Velarde's churches.

Introduction

This book examines the life and work of one of Britain's most gifted church architects, Francis Xavier Velarde (1897–1960). He designed Roman Catholic churches in suburbs and housing estates, mainly around Liverpool and on the Wirral, which enjoyed some recognition in the 1930s and which deserve to be better known. The importance of these churches is perhaps best described by Velarde's friend and obituarist, the architect Herbert Thearle: 'The local ones, beginning in 1927 with St Matthew's at Clubmoor and ending with Holy Cross Birkenhead, 1959, not only brighten the drab parts in which they are to be found but serve to make both spiritually and architecturally aware those who visit.'[1] There was a moment in the 1930s when Velarde was at the forefront of architectural and liturgical thinking in Britain. The war came, and building ceased; by the time it resumed, he had lost his greatest supporter, his former tutor Charles H Reilly, and his work never received the same attention again. Undeterred, Velarde carried on quietly designing churches in his distinctive, increasingly idiosyncratic style. Schools, also at their most radical in the late 1930s, were the financial security of his practice and subsidised the church projects.

Velarde himself wrote little and published less. He set out his thoughts on the profession only once, in an article of 1953 co-authored with his youngest brother Raphael, a parish priest at Bromborough on the Wirral:

> The architect, whom most people regard as an odd and imperious gentleman, producing plans, and commanding that they be translated into brick and stone, has in fact to master and control a hundred practical problems, human and material. He has to keep within a limit of money; he has to compromise, devise, substitute; he has to overcome sudden and unforeseeable difficulties. He has to control all these diverse factors, imposing on them the order of his own design; and out of what may seem at times a conflicting chaos, he has to produce a unified whole. And in the end he has to be content to be misunderstood and misjudged. In a word, he has quite a job.[2]

Lady Chapel, St Teresa's RC church, Upholland

Yet in most ways his career could hardly have been simpler. After graduating in 1925 he spent nearly five years working for an established firm designing churches and schools, then followed that line of work on his own account until his death in 1960. Signing himself 'FXV', but known to his family and friends as Frank and to his tutor Charles H Reilly and fellow students as 'Val', he spent his whole life in and around Liverpool, a family man who served his country, his church and his profession with distinction.[3] It was a good life, lived well and without fuss; a detailed diary or 'log book' that survives for the years 1945–6 describes a loving family and close friendships, good food and a busy workload. Yet this placid appearance covered intense struggles, both physically and in his work. In poor health for most of his adult life, he was an outsider, a Roman Catholic subject to abuse from other professionals (as an insult from a fellow architect recorded in his log book for 1945 relays), a provincial man with a foreign sounding name.[4] In the 1940s he thought of changing it but was dissuaded by his children.

Nikolaus Pevsner, writing in the 1960s and 1970s, admired Velarde's early churches: St. Gabriel's, Blackburn (his one Anglican church, opened in 1933), and St Monica's, Bootle (1936), both came in for high praise. They owe much to European modernism, which Velarde saw at first hand, first on a tour of Germany made with Charles Reilly in 1928 and in extended holidays by car thereafter. However, Pevsner became increasingly dismissive of the post-war churches. Velarde's former pupil, the Polish-born architect Jerzy Faczynski, who himself designed some remarkable churches, offered a more balanced view as early as 1972:

> Professor Pevsner has criticised the top of the tower of St Matthew's Clubmoor – but at the time that church was built [in 1930] there was really only Gothic architecture understood for churches in England – it was a long time still before modern architecture could be accepted, but then many examples had historical items fused into them, like the caryatids in the Highpoint block of flats by Tecton of 1938 ... Now we are beginning to be able to see developments in a historical perspective and I feel that it would be a shame to leave Mr Velarde's work unrecorded.[5]

Velarde's post-war churches, whether small like Our Lady of Pity, Greasby (1952), or substantial in scale, like English Martyrs', Wallasey, of 1953, displayed a confidence in traditional materials that was rapidly going out of fashion in other building types. It is strange to think that these churches are contemporary with the Smithsons' Hunstanton School, or Chamberlin, Powell and Bon's Golden Lane housing. But concerns about being modern never worried Velarde; he was part of a link to an older way of building, preferring evolution to revolution in all things and running only a small

St Monica's RC church, Bootle

St Teresa and the Child Jesus RC church, Borehamwood

Distinctive gold and blue colour scheme to the columns of St Teresa's, Upholland

office, never employing a staff numbering more than 12. The later churches came as a revelation to architectural historians when rediscovered with the listing of St Teresa's, Upholland, in 1999. Holy Cross, Bidston, completed in 1959, was Velarde's personal favourite, and was eventually listed in 2003 after a two-year campaign. It is currently closed and shuttered, but to get inside is to find a riot of colour and craft, full of mosaics and sculpture, while its simple shapes and volumes are almost post-modern. In an unpublished article (perhaps intended as a lecture) that survives in his archive at the University of Liverpool, Velarde gave his own view of criticism:

> We all wish our buildings to be pleasing but many of us are puritanically reluctant to accept a visual pleasure which we cannot explain on extraneous grounds. We are not content merely to be pleased, we must be able to demonstrate that the qualities which rejoice our eyes are good for other reasons. We make great efforts to show that delight proceeds by some necessity from commodity and firmness.[6]

To realise architecture's traditional virtues, ascribed to Henry Wotton in his 1624 translation of Vitruvius's historic tract, Velarde composed his churches out of three key ingredients. The first is fine brickwork. Where funds allowed, he chose two-inch bricks in English Garden Wall bond with matching mortar to create a monolithic appearance as at St Teresa of the Child Jesus, Borehamwood (1959–62). This use of narrow bricks derived from northern Europe, and can be compared with contemporary work by his fellow Liverpudlian Herbert

Rowse, such as the Philharmonic Hall of 1937–9. He devoted one of his few articles to bricks, recording his delight in his diary and hoping that it might become a book.[7] 'In this country where the atmosphere is misty and subtle, the materials which give the best results are those that have a softness as it were in themselves, and blend naturally into the landscape.' He also emphasised the importance of the mortar joints, their shape, size and colour.

The second was colour, especially blue and gold. He loved the colour and lustre of gold – his son Giles recounted how he would travel with a packet of gold leaf in his pocket – and he used gold mosaics on columns, as at St Teresa's, Upholland (1957) and St. Luke's, Pinner (1958), or for crosses set into the floor, as well as leaf to pick out details of carved angels on fonts and altars.

The third was the employment of fine sculptors, first Herbert Tyson Smith and later David John, added an important figurative and humane element to his work. Velarde had a high regard for their skills, perhaps because he came himself to architecture through art school and he retained a lifelong love of drawing. A man of firm views, he wrote of the 'fundamental elements of "Mass, Line and Scale"': 'It is however in these fundamental qualities that so many modern churches fail, sometimes it would seem because the architect is more concerned with such relative incidentals as decoration and ornament, so often trashy, vulgar and cheap – save in terms of money.'[8]

Velarde embraced modernism in the 1930s, but he became acutely aware that the parishioners of his churches liked the familiar, though he sought also to challenge them. He felt that

> The architect's clients – the Priest and People – should be able first of all to trust him; which means something rather different than giving him carte blanche: it implies also intelligent co-operation. They must in addition practise an elementary patience in trying to assimilate his designs, in order that they may understand the reasons which underlie his choice of particular forms.[9]

Confident in his method, the changing currents of contemporary architecture during the 1950s left Velarde undisturbed. No longer distracted by teaching and with the support of family, friends and loyal clients, he produced a series of fine new churches in London and the north-west of England and was immersed in work until shortly before his death in December 1960. He was 63, and even though he carried the effects of injuries from the Great War, a serious car accident in 1932 and bowel cancer in 1940, he might, with better fortune, have expected another decade of productive professional life. Fifty years on, it feels the right moment to evaluate the career of a man celebrated for much of his life, but who was forgotten for many years after his death.

E. Chambré Hardman

1 Velarde's life and career

F X Velarde's background was enigmatic. Velarde is a Spanish name, his father, Julio Velarde (1864–1904), arrived in Liverpool aged five from Chile in the company of a nurse, with his school fees paid via a Panamanian lawyer. The reasons are lost or forgotten.[1] Julio lived with the Rushton family, Cheshire farming folk, and married the 'prettiest daughter', Jane, in 1891, settling in Liverpool and producing six children: four boys and two girls. A noted linguist speaking five languages, he worked as a victualing superintendent and later as a foreign correspondent for the Larrinaga shipping line.[2]

Francis Xavier, born in October 1897, was the fourth child and second son. Called the 'mutt' of the family since, unlike his academic siblings, he was considered to be only good at art, he left St Francis Xavier's College aged 14 and was apprenticed to the merchant navy. Velarde later claimed that by the time he was 16 he had sailed round the world. His son Julian recalled, years later, that 'The docks were a passion of his, especially when there was a sailing clipper unloading, or loading, but really any ship interested him.'[3] The *Architects' Journal* related his love of ships to his feeling for architecture, commenting that 'He has a great love of ships and he delights in the way the design of a ship is composed entirely of practical things.'[4]

At the outbreak of the First World War Velarde tried to join up but, naively giving his true age, he was rejected for being only 17 and sent back to the merchant navy. In 1916, while on leave in Liverpool, he and his elder brother Leo were white-feathered at Exchange Station and duly enlisted; in November 1916 he joined the Royal Naval Division, an army regiment that fought in khaki but which had a naval dress uniform. He was transferred to France in June 1917, where he was gassed at Passchendaele.[5] Velarde was reluctant to talk about the war, save for one story, recounted by Herbert Thearle as an example of Velarde's beguiling mix of naivety and shrewdness. 'He used to tell how he was ordered by a zealous young captain to replace some sandbags at a trench top. The following day, the bags being still untouched, Velarde was commanded once more to do the job but again refused; angrily jumping up himself, the officer fell back with a bullet though his head. "You know", said Velarde, "I'd told him it was dangerous and that it really didn't matter".'[6]

Velarde as 'The Mountaineer', photographed by Edward Chambré Hardman early 1930s

He returned to the lines until frostbite split one of his feet and he was convalescing in England when the armistice was declared. These injuries affected him throughout his life. He found driving difficult and was unable to climb or walk great distances; it is with some irony that his friend the photographer Edward Chambré Hardman used him as the model for a photograph entitled 'The Mountaineer'.

Liverpool School of Architecture

Discharged in 1919, Velarde faced the prospect of no career until his brother Leo paid for him to enrol at the Art School in Liverpool.[7] There his skills as a draughtsman were noticed by Charles Reilly, the larger-than-life head of the School of Architecture at the university, who encouraged him to turn to architecture with the help of a two-year scholarship and direct entry into the second year.[8] Reilly had been looking for willing middle-class students to expand his school, and Velarde fitted the bill. He did well as a student, winning the John Rankin and White Star prizes in 1924 and being shortlisted

Watercolour by Velarde of Stokesay Castle, Shropshire, 1923

for a Rome Scholarship. The Honan Travelling Scholarship (still awarded by the Liverpool Architectural Society) enabled him to study in Paris for six months in 1923.[9]

The appointment of Charles H Reilly (1874–1948) as professor in 1904 had followed the Liverpool School of Architecture's accreditation in 1902, when it became the first university course in architecture to receive the RIBA's validation. It developed a reputation for an academic, Beaux-Arts form of neo-classicism underscored by the city's trans-Atlantic connections. Under Reilly's guidance many students went on to prominence in the profession, all of whom loyally carried the interests of the school with them. Contemporaries of Velarde included William Holford (1907–75), George Checkley (1893–1960), Wesley Dougill (1893–1943) and Edwin Maxwell Fry (1899–1987), as well as his lifelong friends Derek Bridgwater (1899–1983), Bernard Miller (1894–1960) and Herbert Thearle (1903–71). Thearle recalled how the students once played cricket behind the school and broke a lot of windows. 'Charles Reilly soon after sailed into the studio to recover the cost of repairs by collecting cash from each student. ... On he alphabetically went through the studio until, arriving at Velarde, who was busily working away, he asked in a by now very brusque voice indeed, "Cricket in the yard, Velarde?" "I don't mind if I do", was the ingenious reply. So taken aback was the professor that Velarde got off scot free but being no cricketer this was not unfitting.'[10]

Reilly was the most important contact Velarde made at the school, and he became a lifelong mentor. He was adept at identifying promising students and using his considerable influence to assist their careers long after they had left, occasionally taking a hand himself, as when he acted as a consultant on the Peter Jones store in Sloane Square by William Crabtree, another former student. Velarde noted how 'he likes jobs to go to his old schoolmen'.[11] He was a surrogate father figure to many of his most promising students, but Velarde – whose own father had died when he was six – was one of the closest and perhaps his favourite. His support continued long after his retirement in 1933, as witnessed by an exchange from 1938 when Hubert de Cronin Hastings, editor of the *Architects' Journal*, suggested that he moderate the radical political content of a series of articles titled 'Professor Reilly speaks' and instead focus on one or more practitioners. 'I think your idea a very good one provided he is not one of those established old duffers of whom we are all tired. I should like to deal with the younger men ... The sort of people I have in mind are: Velarde, Cachemaille-Day, Chermayeff, Armstrong, Maxwell Fry'.[12] That Velarde was counted in that varied company of modern architects shows the regard in which Reilly held him. Thearle's obituary acknowledged that 'So close were he and Reilly when alive that with his going it seemed that much more of Reilly was lost too.'[13]

9

FXV and Charles Reilly on the balcony of Embassy Court, Brighton, 1934

Starting a practice

Velarde gained his diploma in architecture in 1924, one of the first students to go through the school's new five-year course. However, he did not obtain his full certificate from the RIBA until 1932, perhaps because he had never formally matriculated from St Francis Xavier's College.[14] Upon completing the course he had to choose between working in Liverpool or, in Reilly's words, 'You be a dog and go to America'.[15] Taking Reilly's hint he accepted the offer of a junior, salaried partnership in the practice of Weightman & Bullen. An established Liverpool-based firm with strong connections to the Roman Catholic Church through the Catenian Association of Catholic laymen, most of their projects consisted of churches and schools. Velarde's first project, the design of a cross for the crypt of the Catholic pro-cathedral of St Nicholas Copperas Hill, was produced with Herbert Tyson Smith (1883–1972), a sculptor who had recently come to prominence with a series of local war memorials designed in collaboration with Reilly and other former students. His collaboration with Velarde continued until the late 1950s. But Velarde's role in what briefly became Weightman, Bullen & Velarde was not altogether happy and he complained that he had to 'do all the design work and got paid very little for the trouble'.[16] Even so he took time to undertake a few private commissions, including a lavatory block for St Francis Xavier's College and a house in the nearby suburb of Woolton for Thomas Hague.[17] The house still stands, although much altered.

St Matthew's was Velarde's first substantial project, and as work began on site in 1928 he started teaching part-time at the School of Architecture, which he continued until 1953. He also lectured at St Joseph's Seminary, Upholland, in 1930–1.[18] This was a critical period in the formation of his architectural style. In 1928 he accompanied Reilly to Germany, driving down the Rhine to see the Pressa exhibition in Cologne, churches in Frankfurt and an exhibition of modern housing, the *Weissenhofseidlung* in Stuttgart. Velarde preserved souvenirs and photographs of this trip for the rest of his life and

Velarde relaxes in a bar on his Rhineland tour, 1928

the influences of German expressionist architecture, such as Paul Bonatz's railway station in Stuttgart and the churches of Dominikus Böhm and Martin Weber, came through in his designs once he had a free hand in determining his style.

In 1930, with St Matthew's nearing completion, Velarde ended his relationship with Weightman & Bullen and set up his own practice. An old school friend, Canon John Francis, responsible for acquiring sites in the Liverpool diocese, commissioned Our Lady of Lourdes School in Southport with the explanation that 'I want you, FXV, to build this school. I don't like Weightman and Bullen'.[19] Later that year, St Matthew's opened to favourable reviews. With connections established among the Liverpool Catholic clergy, one well-publicised church and the security of part-time teaching, Velarde could pursue his own architectural ambitions, developing ideas he had seen in Germany. Late in 1930 he entered the competition for the new Anglican

Velarde's unplaced entry for the Guildford Cathedral competition, 1931

Velarde and Madge shortly after meeting, Marlow, 1929

Velarde with his sons Julian (right) and Giles, showing his bandaged feet, unrecovered from the effects of trenchfoot, *c* 1935

cathedral in Guildford. His brick design submitted in 1931 was similar in massing to Edward Maufe's winning entry, but was unplaced.

In 1929 Velarde met his future wife Madge Curran (1910–90), born in Buckinghamshire to parents of Liverpool origin and a student at Manchester University; they were introduced by her architect cousin Joseph P Alcock (1905–66).[20] They married in 1930, and rented a flat from the university at No 3 Abercromby Square. Juggling family life with a growing practice and part-time teaching was made easier by living so close to the architecture school at No 25. There were two sons of the marriage: Julian (1932–2005), who studied architecture and joined his father's practice despite never completing his formal qualifications, and Giles (1935–) who became an artist and a leading exhibition designer. Julian described how the family lived on the top two floors of the house, with the office on the floors below. After Giles was born, Velarde purchased No 7a Abercromby Square as a home, for £1,095, retaining No 3 as an office. He had earlier bought a farmhouse in the

Langdales, a particularly beautiful part of the Lake District, as a wedding present for Madge, which they used as a holiday home.[21] 'Wholly engrossed in his work, he does not believe an architect can have a full social or athletic life and remain an architect in the true sense of the word', was a later but perceptive comment from the *Architects' Journal*.[22]

A reputation for brick churches

The early 1930s saw Velarde design two of his most significant churches – St Gabriel's, Blackburn, and St Monica's, Bootle – one Anglican and one Roman Catholic. But between these projects, in September 1932, he suffered a serious accident, when he was hit by a lorry while trying to fix the petrol gauge of his Armstrong Siddeley saloon car outside a garage in Gloucestershire. Because he was hanging half out of the passenger seat, he sustained a seriously broken leg, which required two operations (leading in turn to heart trouble) and a year of recuperation. Velarde reported that he lost commissions for St Robert Bellarmine, Bootle, and St John the Evangelist, New Ferry, churches realised by other architects, as well as his regular school work. It was only Reilly's intervention, negotiating a continuation of his teaching salary as a loan, which allowed him to employ Joe Alcock as an assistant and to secure the practice's survival.[23]

St Gabriel's, Blackburn, was Velarde's only building for the Anglican Church. It is sometimes described as a collaboration with his friend Bernard Miller, whose father was a canon of the Church of England and who specialised in designing progressive Anglican churches.[24] Giles Velarde recalled his father's explanation that the evangelical congregation and vicar had been nervous of employing a young Catholic architect with a foreign-sounding name, and that the two architects agreed that each would produce a sketch scheme. After Velarde's was chosen, Miller served as a notional consultant without any animosity.[25] A contemporary account in the *Manchester Guardian* gives no suggestion that Miller produced detailed proposals, but confirms that he and Reilly supported Velarde's commission.[26] St Gabriel's cost £15,000, and upon completion in 1933 received positive reviews by Edward Maufe and Charles Reilly in the architectural press.[27] Reilly compared Velarde favourably with Miller, despite both being his ex-pupils: 'Velarde's is the more original and daring spirit, in that he will trust to the utmost simplicity, such as in the exterior of his church of St Gabriel's at Blackburn, or in that little temporary altar and chancel in the church of Our Lady of Lourdes at Southport, and out of nothing, as it were, produce a compelling and moving composition essentially religious'.[28]

Opposite: The tower of St Gabriel's, Blackburn, photographed by Edward Chambré Hardman shortly after completion

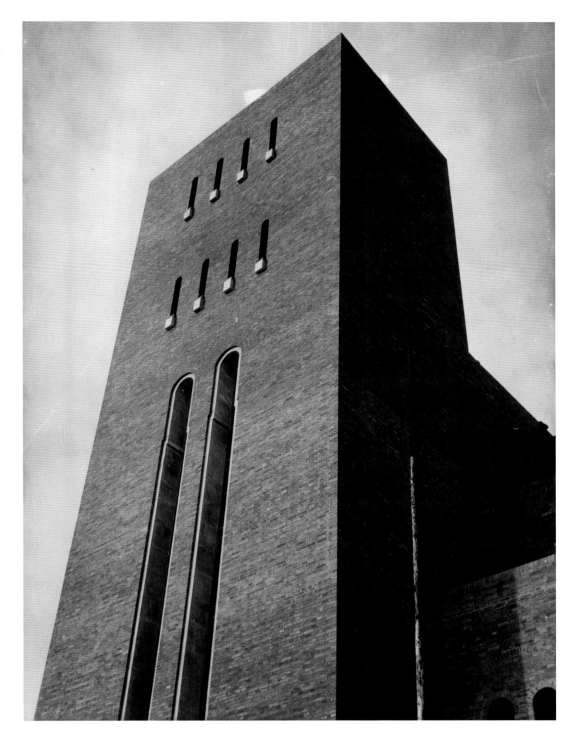

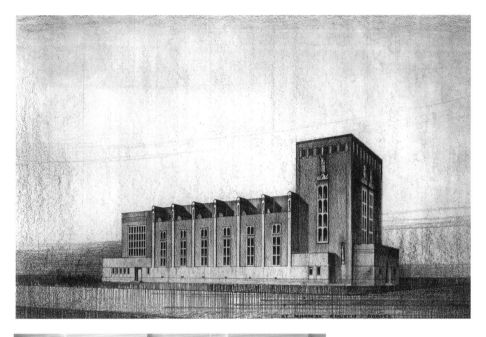

Velarde's perspective of St
Monica's, Bootle

Angel detail carved by
W L Stevenson to designs by
Velarde for the reredos of St
Monica's, Bootle

St Monica's, Bootle, confirmed Velarde's reputation without Reilly's assistance. Completed in 1936, it is a powerful and simple rectangular brick box with a dominant *Westwerk* presided over by three angels carved by Herbert Tyson Smith. Nikolaus Pevsner called it 'an epoch-making church for England', much influenced by the Modern Movement of Continental Europe and particularly the work of Dominikus Böhm.[29] All trace of the Byzantine influences of St Matthew's was banished in favour of a brick expressionism that was tinged with the architect's own idiosyncrasies.

The integration of art and architecture was a constant theme in Velarde's career, and at St Monica's he worked closely with artists to ensure a wholly coherent composition. He made the initial designs himself and established a close team of collaborators to realise his ideas. Velarde won the RIBA's Godwin and Wimperis bursary in 1937. He loaded his red 1928 Gordon England 'Cup' Austin 7 and headed down through France to Switzerland,

Velarde on holiday in the South of France, 1958

visiting August Perret's church at Le Raincy and Karl Moser's church of St Anthony in Basel.[30] In 1939 he returned to Switzerland to see Fritz Metzger's modernist church of St Charles Borromeo of 1933 at Lucerne. Family holidays were often accompanied by Edward Chambré Hardman, known as 'Hardy', although Madge Velarde complained about the amount of photographic equipment he packed into the small car. She learned to drive during the war, and thereafter Velarde himself drove little. In the 1950s they took long holidays through France to Spain, a country of fascination for Velarde with his Spanish roots, and he always took a sketch book and diary to record things of interest.

By 1938 Velarde's practice was firmly established, earning glowing reviews in the Catholic magazine *Art Notes*, of which Reilly was a patron. The cover of its January–February 1938 issue featured an axonometric of his Our Lady of Lourdes Catholic Primary School in Southport. Reilly's verdict

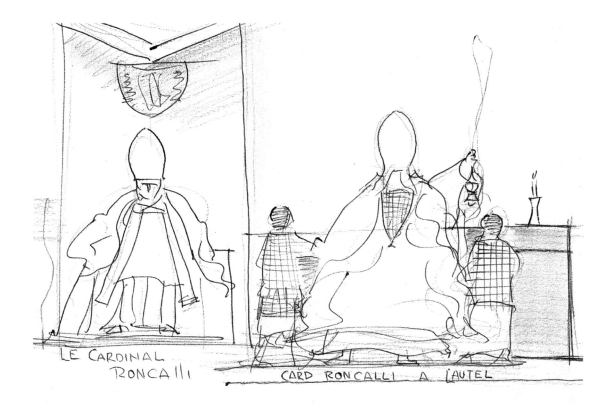

Front and rear elevations of Cardinal Roncalli (the future Pope John XXIII), from Velarde's sketch-books, 1958

was unequivocal. 'Most modern work is frankly, even crudely revolutionary. Velarde's is something better. It belongs to both the present and the past, and I think the future as well'.[31] The financial security generated by the school commisions enabled time to be lavished upon the churches.

Expanding the practice

Like so many architects who set up practice in the 1930s, the war deprived Velarde of a decade of architectural activity just as he was getting into his stride. The family evaded the bombing of Liverpool by moving to the suburban seaside safety of Formby in 1940, while the office and teaching remained in Abercromby Square. Velarde came to enjoy the half-hour train journey as a time for reflection, expressing irritation in his log books when he had to spend it in conversation with friends and family. However, in 1940 he became so seriously ill with bowel cancer that the last rites were administered.[32] Alongside detailed records in his log books of his sleep patterns and bowel movements, Velarde also worried that 'my eyes bother me very much and although I see all light and colour and shapes in a confused mass, detail, except I look with one eye, is lost to me'. This may explain why his later churches became simpler in shape and brighter in colour.[33]

Yet by 1944 Velarde was sufficiently well to participate in 'The Church and the Artist', a conference at Chichester Cathedral. He was one of 21 attendees, who also included Dorothy Sayers, Henry Moore, T S Eliot, Duncan Grant and Edward Maufe, the only other architect present. The invitation came through his reputation for church designs and a personal connection with the Bishop of Chichester, for whom he had designed a silver cross, one of nine made by Tyson Smith that year. Times were hard and new ideas were needed. Sir Eric Maclagen, director of the British Museum, pointed out that even Christopher Wren had been made to build on the cheap and his interiors had been sometimes added later; he advocated some form of mass production. Henry Moore was uncompromising; his work followed its own path, which was not necessarily that of the church. T S Eliot thought that the religious dramatist should make his characters as real as the ordinary people he met. Dorothy Sayers was blunt; the church had to address three levels of intelligence at once: '(1) unspoilt children or peasants, (2) those in the Darwinian stage, (3) those who apprehended the modern physicist position'.[34] Velarde stood apart. Later he wrote that the architect should himself be an artist, for whom 'tradition is the lifeblood of art … it is his function to combine tradition and creativeness, which are not opposed but, rightly understood, are complementary and even integral to each other'.[35] His dissenting conservatism was at odds with the progressive mood of the conference, yet growing out of step with the world seemed never to have troubled him.

Silver cross, one of nine made in 1944 by Herbert Tyson Smith to Velarde's design. This is the same motif Tyson Smith used on Velarde's gravestone carved in 1961

War brought a further modernist influence to the environment at Liverpool University with the arrival in 1941 of a Polish School of Architecture, organised by Wladyslaw Sikorski, the Prime Minister and Commander-in-Chief in exile. This European influx, headed by Colonel Ladislaw Torun, required the rather parochial English to 'run to catch up'.[36] One of the Polish students, Jerzy Faczynski, recalled that Velarde's habit of giving short lectures, due to his poor health, was unexpectedly appreciated, for 'he spoke very slowly, and here was a speaker we could understand with his little lectures lasting about 15 minutes'.[37]

As the country emerged from war, Velarde re-engaged in practice with fresh energy, dashing between meetings with priests, local authority directors of education, site meetings, student reviews and lectures. His surviving log books from the years 1945–8 make exhausting reading. The entry for 22 October 1945 declared that 'it is the beginning of a new period of work and work to your choice is one of the lasting pleasures of life'.[38] His first assistant, in June 1946, was John Robinson, who he took on as an apprentice, to be followed by a Miss Bland. The supervision of final-year theses enabled him to identify the best students and offer them employment on graduation. In 1947 he took on Gerald Beech (1921–2013), Jan Peter de Waal and (briefly) Quentin Hughes (1920–2004).[39] Janet Gnosspelius (1926–2010), a family friend of Arthur Ransome and a model for his character Nancy Blackett in *Swallows and Amazons*, first joined the practice as a year-out student in 1947.[40] She also ran the office; a natural pedant, she was ruthless with corrections to spelling in correspondence.[41]

Liverpool's population has the largest percentage of Roman Catholics of any city in Great Britain, thanks to its importance as an international port and to Irish immigration in the 19th century. A see was created in 1850 but only the Lady Chapel and chancel chapels of E W Pugin's intended cathedral were built before funding was diverted to meet the urgent demand for schools. The cathedral project was revived by Richard Downey, Archbishop of Liverpool, who envisaged the city as a Catholic powerhouse second only to Rome. A century after Catholic emancipation, in 1929, he acquired the site of the city's workhouse on Brownlow Hill and commissioned Sir Edwin Lutyens to produce a personal version of Byzantine classicism, replete with a central dome of greater diameter than that of St Peter's in Rome. He even raised £1 million, secured locally and from the United States, a third of the estimated cost when construction began in 1933.[42] Velarde's first comments on Lutyens's scheme were carefully ambivalent, telling the *Liverpool Post* in 1938 that 'a traditional form being required, no happier choice of style could have been made'.[43] Work ceased in 1940, however, and by 1945 inflation had pushed the cost to nearly £30 million. Charles Reilly, acting for Thomas Adamson, private secretary to Archbishop Downey, invited Velarde to complete the building to a reduced design, but he refused. He found himself avoiding a disappointed Reilly, after the professor had been left with no option but to recommend Adrian Gilbert Scott, brother of Sir Giles. The stressful situation prompted Velarde to set out the reasons for his decision:

> I do not wish to give the major part of my life to carrying out another's design especially when I am not convinced of the suitability of the design.

> I feel I would be at a disadvantage with the committee which might impose too much on a local man.

> My conviction that to build a church larger than St Peter's Rome, in such a provincial area + at such great price, is in very bad taste. A very much more modest structure could likewise accommodate the Catholic population + be more in the Christian spirit + be more beautiful.[44]

When in 1953 Scott published his scaled-down version of Lutyens's scheme, the result was roundly criticised as weak and Velarde felt vindicated in his decision. By 1959 it was clear that even this was too expensive, and Archbishop Heenan held a new competition, won the next year by Frederick Gibberd with the 'wigwam' design finally built in 1962–7.

Building for Shrewsbury Diocese

Before 1939, Velarde's projects had almost all been for the Catholic Archdiocese of Liverpool. After 1945, however, the adjacent diocese of Shrewsbury, which extended to the Wirral, became a prolific source of new work. His brother Ralph was appointed parish priest to Christ the King, Bromborough, in April 1945, but a more important patron was his old school friend Fr John Murphy, who as parish priest of Our Lady of Pity, Greasby, first approached Velarde in 1944 about the possibility of a new church to replace an old army hut that his congregation had been using for services.[45] By the time Father Murphy opened the church in July 1952, he had been elevated as Bishop of Shrewsbury. He went on in 1961 to become Archbishop of Cardiff, where he was known by the epithet 'the builder' because of the extensive school and church construction programme he sponsored.[46]

Although not a large building, the Greasby church has gravitas. The use of a campanile, linked to the body of the church by an arcade, and low aisle-less interiors spanned by Romanesque brick arches gave a sense of grandeur that belied its small size. It was economical, stylish and successful: at least seven more churches followed in the Diocese of Shrewsbury, including the imposing English Martyrs, Wallasey, in 1951–3, the petite St Cuthbert by the Forest, Mouldsworth, in 1952–5, St Gabriel's, Alsager, in 1953–5, St Mary Magdalene, Much Wenlock, in 1955, Holy Cross, Bidston, in 1957–9, and two in Shrewsbury itself: St Winefrede's in 1956–7 and Our Lady of Pity in 1959–61. The designs for these last two were so similar that the client is said to have asked for a reimbursement of a percentage of the architect's fee.[47] We have no record of Velarde's reply. Other projects for Shrewsbury diocese included reworking the chapel at the convent of Our Lady of Sion, Acton Burnell, and schools including St Bede's, Handbridge, Chester, and Holy Cross, Bidston, both largely designed in 1947.

The 1950s were a busy time for the practice, with Jan P de Waal and Frank Brown taking on much of the school work and Janet Gnosspelius running many of the church projects, always under Velarde's close eye. He was always very careful to control the details of the churches, insisting on selecting the colour scheme and frequently designing the altarware.[48] He recognised that some details were best decided on site rather than in lengthy discussions at the office. Brown and Gnosspelius recalled that

> he used to love to draw a sketch of a small detail in the pile of sand, with his stick, on the job – a habit which, if rain was coming on, could

West front of Our Lady of Pity, Greasby, drawn by Velarde

be difficult for the foreman, but Tommy Henshaw, foreman at Holy Cross School, Bidston, would deal with this by having the precious detail immediately covered with a tarpaulin held down with bricks at the corners and so preserved for use, and for the inspection by the quantity surveyor as evidence of the architect's instruction.[49]

The increase in workload and Liverpool University (the landlord) requiring No 3 Abercromby Square for other uses resulted in the office moving to Windsor Buildings, Great George Street, in the city centre in 1952. It was at this time that Velarde finally gave up his part-time teaching. Velarde's post-war churches became far more colourful, with dramatic uses of gold or silver contrasted with orange and blue. However, he urged caution, writing that

In a church of modern design it will be wise to avoid elaborate colour schemes; three colours will usually prove sufficient, and the scheme will find its natural climax in the decoration of the sanctuary. Generally speaking, quiet colouring of the walls will offer a splendid foil to a more elaborate pattern in the treatment of roof or ceiling; and the sanctuary floor offers an obvious opportunity for a design in harmony with the altar.[50]

Janet Gnosspelius recalled how

Velarde … would take any amount of trouble to get just the effect he wanted. He was very sensitive to colour. He made a point of doing any sketches to indicate to his client the colour scheme he had in mind (for a sanctuary for instance) with his own hand, not trusting it to any assistant. Again he was very sensible about not deciding on the exact shade of the colour in advance but making his final decision from samples in the light in which they would be seen, putting himself to a good deal of trouble to visit a job several times in a week until he was satisfied that the painters were doing just what he wanted.[51]

Continuity and diversion

Projects of this period were not confined to the Shrewsbury diocese. Two fine churches were built in the Liverpool Archdiocese: St Teresa's, Upholland, in 1952–7 – a smaller version of English Martyrs – and St Alexander's, Bootle, built in 1955–7; demolished in 1991, it is perhaps the greatest loss among Velarde's churches. A more idiosyncratic, one-off building was the bijou Shrine of Our Lady of Lourdes, Blackpool, 1955–7, commissioned as a memorial thanksgiving chapel for the relatively light bombing taken by the Diocese of Lancaster during the Second World War.[52] In a departure for Velarde, this chapel was entirely faced in Portland stone and featured sculpture by the ecclesiastical artist David John, then only in his mid-twenties, Tyson Smith being too busy. Described as 'a Velarde discovery', he replaced Tyson Smith as Velarde's principal sculptor, despite some misgivings about John's artistic judgement, although he was very good technically.[53]

The sculptor Neville Bertram, who worked on early school projects, recalled disparagingly that 'Velarde had no drawing skill and left the creative element to Tyson Smith', after producing sketches 'on the back of an old envelope'.[54] This is a harsh assessment of the architect, who while not a draughtsman of the highest order, was nevertheless a keen sketcher and very capable of producing elegant drawings. It is likely that having worked closely together on many of the fittings for St Matthew's and St Monica's churches, he and Tyson Smith understood each other's requirements from quick and rudimentary communications. They remained lifelong friends.[55]

Velarde himself loved drawing and painting, as shown in his log book when he took a day out to produce an angel and child or a Madonna for stained glass, but he rarely had time to take it seriously.[56] As Herbert Thearle explained, 'To all his projects he gave more personal attention than variable health really permitted and although some of his detailed drawings were slight it used to be uplifting to see them taking shape in the studios and shops of the craftsmen he enlisted.' If Velarde was not happy he would take the commission elsewhere; 'old associations and even friendships would be waived if he believed – as he often did – the job could be bettered by going elsewhere'.[57]

A still more unusual commission was an advisory role in the design of the Basilica of St Pius x at Lourdes. This vast underground concrete church, designed for a congregation of 25,000 people, was opened in 1958 to mark the centenary of the Lourdes apparitions. It was designed by Pierre Vago, assisted by the engineer Eugene Freyssinet, and overseen by an international design committee of six architects under the leadership of Gio Ponti. Velarde was

Side elevation of Our Lady of Lourdes Shrine, Blackpool

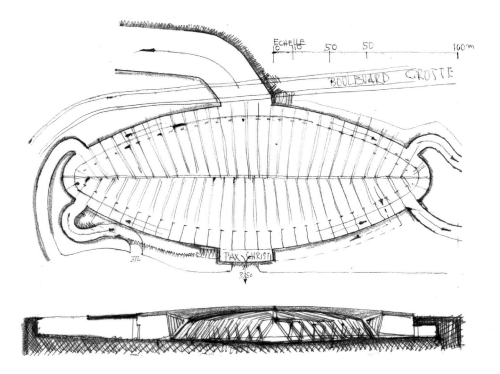

Velarde's sketch of the plan of the Basilica of St Pius x at Lourdes designed by Pierre Vago, when he served as part of an international team led by Gio Ponti

the United Kingdom's representative, recommended by Archbishop Godfrey to Pierre-Marie Théas, Bishop of Tarbes and Lourdes.[58] He visited the site in 1954, twice in 1955 and again in 1956, adding the stop to the long holidays taken with Madge by car to Spain, and attended the official opening in March 1958. He confided a lively description to his holiday diary:

> The Abri has little natural light, which pleased me. The roof is like an inverted fish's spine forming a ribbed canopy. A great tent without columns, riding over a vast space 200′ × 618′ approximately. In the subdued light the coarse colour of the concrete and its texture are not apparent and the whole effect is majestic and the space full of mystery. ... The space is vast. Scores of people are all focused on the High Altar. Twice the population of Formby could be comfortably seated and all would see. The floor in concrete slopes heavily. The great ambulatory is wide – 30′ – like a road and circumvents the whole interior. This building will affect all over Europe and the world. With normal fenestration I think

it might fail to be so effective. The majesty of the naked fabric should be preserved. But the temptation to decorate will arise. The only décor should, I think, be primitive frescoes, such as at the 12th century church in Ville Neuve de Marsan, of blessed memory, or mosaics as at Ravenna.[59]

The description evokes much of Velarde's love of simple, powerful spaces. For his pains he received an OBE in 1957, of which Janet Gnosspelius recounted a story typical of his humility. 'The Queen said: "What have you received this honour for?" – FXV: "I really don't know".'[60]

For Westminster

Velarde's work for the Diocese of Westminster began with a small chapel for the Grail, an ecumenical women's society who owned an old farmhouse in the London suburb of Pinner. It is a single-storey brick building, externally almost unadorned but with characteristic Velarde windows; the humble interior displays his characteristic eye for colour and detail. The simple space and altar are some of his most elegant work.

On the back of this project the nearby church of St Luke's was secured from Fr Wilfrid Trotman, who had studied at the Royal College of Music before his ordination, and who was an organist and composer. He saw the church as a complete piece of art, where the contents and their enclosure were as one, declaring to the *Catholic Herald* in 1958 that 'while I live, and am here, I'll have no "repository" art invading this church. Nothing will go in it that has not the approval of the architect'.[61] Such views chimed well with Velarde's, as did Fr Trotman's recognition that furniture and fittings inherited from other churches could detract from the coherence of a new building, as had happened at St Cuthbert's, Mouldsworth. Here was a perfect client. The Archbishop of Westminster, Cardinal Godfrey, had a reputation for conservatism in church architecture and intervened if he felt a design was too radical, but having previously (1953–6) been Archbishop of Liverpool, he recognised that Velarde had become a well-established and safe pair of hands.[62]

The success at Pinner led to three other churches in the diocese: St Teresa of the Child Jesus, Borehamwood, designed from 1959 and completed in 1962; St Vincent, Potters Bar of 1960–2 (demolished); and St Edmund of Canterbury at Whitton, Twickenham, designed in 1960 and built in 1961–3. These were finished by Janet Gnosspelius, Julian Velarde and Richard O'Mahony after Velarde's sudden death in December 1960. They carried the hallmark of Velarde in their overall form and decoration, but display a slightly awkward process of transition towards modernism.

A clear break with the traditional London designs can be seen in the last church in which Velarde had some involvement. He produced designs in early

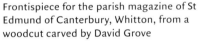

Frontispiece for the parish magazine of St Edmund of Canterbury, Whitton, from a woodcut carved by David Grove

West front of St Edmund of Canterbury, Whitton

1960 for St Michael and All Angels, Woodchurch, near Birkenhead, in 1960, but the scheme was then revised by Richard O'Mahony, who had not long graduated from Liverpool University. The church, built in 1964–5, marks a fundamental shift from the linear nave suggested by Velarde's sketches to a centralised plan under a pyramidal roof. This solution is all O'Mahony. He continued the practice after Velarde's death as the F X Velarde Partnership, producing such interesting churches as St Patrick's, Clinkham Wood, St Helens, in 1963–4 before dropping the Velarde name after Julian and his wife Patricia (née Moores) moved to London.

Velarde's untimely death in December 1960 was traumatic personally and professionally for the practice. The office had employed a number of highly talented graduates, had worked with regarded artists from all fields, yet the church projects from which its reputation largely stemmed remained resolutely the crafted output of one man's vision. But times were changing. The architectural competition for Liverpool Metropolitan Cathedral early in 1960 had produced not just a radically different solution with Frederick

Gibberd's winning entry but had seen the majority of the shortlisted schemes forego a linear nave.[63] Velarde had been pressured into entering. His solution to liturgical developments was considered one of the best by reviewers, but ill health had resulted in an uncharacteristically poor set of drawings and the scheme was passed over.[64] Liverpool Metropolitan Cathedral was not destined to be his legacy.

The list of idiosyncratic churches left by Velarde has been diminished through demolition and damaged through careless alteration, while his personal favourite, Holy Cross, Bidston, is currently unused and vulnerable. Those that remain accessible, however, serve as a powerful reminder of the impact a careful architect with a passion for his projects can achieve.

COMPOSITION OF
ELEMENTS

2 European influences and the 'other modern'

Velarde's drawing ability brought him to architecture, rather than personal interest or family connections, but the young man who graduated in 1924 appeared a self-reliant professional, albeit a provincial one. When he was a student, the Liverpool University School of Architecture followed the Beaux-Arts method of teaching, strong in the logistics of classical planning and the study of the orders. On his return in 1928 to take a part-time teaching post, he found it in flux, both in what was being taught and because of the state of architecture more widely. It was a second and more personal education at this time that led him to develop as an original architect.

Despite his wartime and merchant navy experiences, Velarde had seen little architecture abroad. Before World War One the international focus at the school had been defined by the aphorism 'Reilly does America, Adshead does Europe', reflecting the influences of the respective schools of architecture and town planning.[1] But by the late 1920s a growing awareness of European developments was being driven by a younger generation of architecture graduates, including Edwin Maxwell Fry, William Holford and John Hughes. Hughes, winner of a gold medal in the art competition of the Olympic Games in 1932 with a design for a 'Sports and Recreation Centre with Stadium' for Liverpool, worked in Liverpool City Council's Housing Department from 1930 where, as Lancelot Keay's deputy, he was responsible for the shift from neo-Georgian housing to walk-up apartment blocks in a modern, streamlined style. It is too simple to think of architecture as a straight fight between neo-classicism and modernism. Both were equally evident by 1930, the latter considered suitable for factories and the occasional house, and the former for public buildings and offices. Churches lay outside such conventions.

There was, however, another route, which the historian Gavin Stamp called an 'alternative modernism', and it is here where we should position Velarde's work.[2] The early modernism of northern Europe is distinguished by its fine brickwork and balance of light and shade, areas of fenestration balanced by blind walling and by the massing of blocks of contrasting

Composition of elements, study by Velarde as a student, 1923 heights and shapes, sometimes referred to as expressionism. Examples include Stockholm Town Hall by Ragnar Östberg (1911–23), Hilversum Town Hall by Willem Dudok (1924–31), Gruntvig's Church by Peder Vilhelm Jensen Klint (1913–40) in Copenhagen, and many churches along and around the Rhine valley, notably by Dominikus Böhm (1880–1955), Martin Weber (1890–1941) and Rudolf Schwarz (1897–1961). It was to the Rhineland that Velarde travelled in 1928 in the company of Charles Reilly.

Before 1928, Velarde's principal project had been St Matthew's, Clubmoor, where the brief had called for a Byzantine style. The exotic Byzantine idiom had become the legitimate alternative to the more monumental Romanesque for Roman Catholic churches in the United Kingdom following the opening of J F Bentley's Westminster Cathedral in 1903; it was seen by Cardinal Vaughan as representing the earliest phase of Christian architecture and therefore more authentic than Gothic.[3] The austere internal brickwork of Westminster Cathedral, left exposed where the decoration remained uncompleted, was much admired by younger architects and in 1924 Professor Reilly claimed that its 'lofty plain wall surfaces, even of common stock brick, were more important in giving the idea of remoteness and seclusion from the world than the richest clustered Gothic columns'.[4] From this it was a short step to the still greater simplicity of modernism towards which Reilly began to turn by the late 1920s.

Velarde wrote an article on 'Modern church architecture' sometime probably in the late 1920s. Never published, though perhaps given as a lecture, it displays great enthusiasm for this changing mood.

In England we normally build on a small scale and small-scale art of any kind cannot contain more than one vital interest without confusion. Simplicity is the elementary quality of all great art as of all greatness …

It is precisely in this respect that modern architecture gains merit – the form, the mass is now seen properly related to detail, site and surroundings. Your modern architect is not concerned with a form of historic detail about which to hang his building, but is concerned that planes and masses of surface should be arranged in harmony or in dramatic and elegant contrast.

Modern architecture is interesting in its comparison with other kinds as it seems to select so intelligently the good qualities of each age, using them with a fine discrimination. It takes the classic ideal of purity of line and simplicity of detail – the Norman strength of mass when character demands it. The elegance of early Renaissance art can be matched and balanced and the colour and the fervour of mediaeval art obtained.

Externally the lines may be severe, while inside soft or dramatic colouring may be arranged.[5]

Velarde's idea of modernism at this stage is a stripped-down monumentality, very much in key with Stamp's 'alternative modernism', but suggesting that he had not yet visited Germany. He made a telling contrast between the work of northern Europe and more southern countries, in which he included France and Germany. 'The north European type has been applied with great success to all types of building including the monumental', including Sir Giles Gilbert Scott's Liverpool Anglican Cathedral, which he considered 'perhaps the greatest contribution to present day English architecture. Critics can denounce whole aspects of it, but the fundamental quality of freshness combined with its truly sculpturesque modelling, plus a proper discrimination in the choice and handling of materials has never been surpassed'. It is easy to study the foreign influences on Reilly and his acolytes, and to forget that one of the most powerful examples of 'alternative modernism' was going up in their midst; Scott also taught part-time at the School of Architecture. Velarde felt that 'Scott's work lacks the warmth of humanity, it is if anything too controlled, too mechanical.'[6] He was also critical of Auguste Perret and most German architecture, singling out only Ludwig Ruff (1878–1934) and the Czech Josef Gočár (1880–1945). His greatest praise was reserved for Ivor Tengbom, the Swedish architect 'already universally known for his masterpiece the Högalid Church. It is considered wonderfully beautiful. His ability to model on most satisfying lines is equalled by his colour sense'.[7] Built in 1916–23, the Högalid Church (Högalidskyrkan) was claimed by Edward Maufe to be the European church to have the greatest single influence on modern English ecclesiastical architecture.[8]

The early 20th century saw the Nordic countries belatedly industrialise, and the growth of their major cities with brick buildings that ranged from expressions of national romanticism to a gentle neo-classicism. Velarde never visited Scandinavia, yet his archive contains several photographs and a detailed description of the Engelbrekt Church (Engelbrektskyrkan) in Stockholm, completed in 1914 to the designs of Lars Wahlman. Despite the very great difference in scale, there are similarities between this church and Velarde's proposed church of Our Lady of Lourdes in Southport, and still more with the work of Wahlman's contemporary, Ferdinand Boberg (1860–1946).

After St Matthew's, Velarde re-evaluated his approach, and while still designing expansive walls of brickwork punctuated by small windows he took out the historical motifs, creating a form of stripped-down Byzantine which he would make his own. This change in style correlated to the journey he made through the Rhineland in 1928 with Reilly.

Second study for Our Lady of Lourdes RC church, Hillside, Southport, 1930

Velarde's archive contains photographs of the Pressa exhibition in Cologne and the *Wiessenhofseidlung* in Stuttgart, the highlights of this visit. The International Press Exhibition, known as Pressa, held in 1928 was an exposition of modern printing, publishing and advertising set along three kilometres of the east bank of the River Rhine at Cologne. It was a response to the 1925 Exposition des Arts Décoratifs et Industriels Modernes in Paris and an opportunity for Germany, newly readmitted into the international fold, to display its abilities in the fields of design and architecture.[9] The main building complex comprised a series of largely permanent, traditional, brick-clad structures, including a 42-metre-high tower for Café Hag, all designed by the director of urban planning at Cologne, Alfred Abel. Their symmetrical compositions with plain brick facades and steep-pitched roofs set up a strong formal geometry for the whole site into which individual press and trade pavilions were inserted. Here we have alternative visions of the modern – adjacent, yet assiduously ignoring each other. They included a trade pavilion by Erich Mendelsohn for the publisher Rudolf Mosse; a modernist 'House of Nations' for international exhibitors; and, at one end of the long main avenue, a steel-framed church by the specialist ecclesiastical architect Otto Bartning. This was a curious if dramatic hybrid with a modern structure of steel and glass used to produce a monumental, symmetrical *Westwerk*. Comparisons can be made between this *Westwerk* and contemporary brick churches in and around Cologne by Dominikus Böhm and Rudolf Schwarz.

The highlight was the Soviet Pavilion by El Lissitzky, a constructivist tour-de-force which made a noted contrast to the staid and traditional British pavilion. *Das Berliner Tageblatt* commented on the difference between the Soviet Pavilion and the British exhibition organised by M Neven du Mont:

> Everything that separates the two finds expression when one sees the two brought together under the same roof. England: pious, aristocratic, historically reverent, at peace in its confidence ... And Russia; one must admit, grandeur in its exposition of social conditions, with really mechanical equipment, conveyor belts of great cubistic zig-zags; causing a stir by its enormous steps of progress which are depicted in bold and bragging manner, always in glaring red. Forward![10]

Near Cologne is Mönchengladbach, where Dominikus Böhm's St Kamillus was nearing completion. Did Velarde visit this? In Frankfurt Reilly and Velarde visited churches by both Böhm and Weber. We cannot be certain of Velarde's itinerary, but there are parallels between Böhm's work and early designs made in 1932 for his second church, St Gabriel's, Blackburn, notably in Mönchengladbach's entrance, defined by a deeply recessed and exaggerated vertical slot set against a blank façade of flat brick. Böhm's influence is even more obvious in Velarde's next church, St Monica's, Bootle, where Pevsner cited as possible sources Böhm's St Joseph's, Hindenburg, and the Caritas Institute at Cologne-Hohenlind, as well as St Kamillus, Mönchengladbach.[11] After the war, Velarde occasionally repeated this

Westwerk of St Kamillus, Mönchengladbach, by Dominikus Böhm

Drawing of the first scheme for St Gabriel's, Blackburn

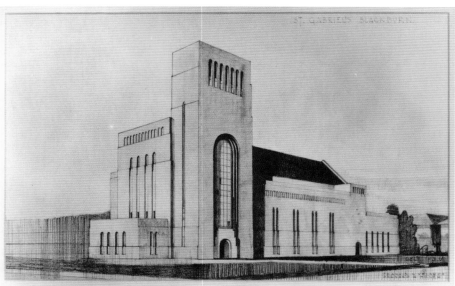

Charcoal sketch
of Christ the King,
Leverkusen, by
Dominikus Böhm

Distinctive Velarde
window arrays
to side aisle of St
Luke's, Pinner

Church interior, charcoal sketch by Dominikus Böhm

great block of west-end masonry, principally on his London churches. The recessed staggered brickwork used by Böhm at Christ the King, Leverkusen, in 1928 also appeared in Velarde's first scheme for St Gabriel's, Blackburn. In addition to the parallels in detail and massing, the plan form at Leverkusen, with small asymmetrical side aisles set off against a much larger rectangular nave, was much employed by Velarde after 1928. One more feature was inspired by Böhm: rectangular panels of round-headed windows, again noted by Pevsner.[12] First employed at St Monica's, the motif became ubiquitous in Velarde's churches, in thin panels along a nave or in larger arrays to the side of the sanctuary.

The *Weissenhofsiedlung* in Stuttgart, built in 1927, was an entirely modernist suburb developed by the Deutsche Werkbund that included buildings by Walter Gropius, Hans Scharoun and Le Corbusier. Here there was no traditionalist foil. Their visit might have had more impact upon Reilly than Velarde, as it was perhaps the moment the professor's interest turned away from neo-classicism. Velarde preserved souvenirs and photographs of this trip for the rest of his life, but he may have been most impressed by the massive masonry central station in Stuttgart, of 1914–28 by Paul Bonatz. This recently completed building had something of a church in its appearance with its tall clock tower, a long foyer 'nave', great 'west window' and asymmetrical stacked masonry. Bonatz was part of *Der Blok*, an association of architects founded in 1928 to counter the avant-garde *Der Ring* founded two years earlier by Hugo Häring and Mies van der Rohe. Several members of *Der Ring* had been involved in the *Weissenhofsiedlung* and their overt modernist presence in Stuttgart, where Bonatz was head of the School of Architecture, was seen as highly provocative.

Der Blok's manifesto included an overtly critical review of international modernism as 'A too hasty advertising activity for fashionable products, which must jeopardize a healthy development'.[13] Instead its architects sought to modernise historical (and generally masonry) forms through simplification rather than revolutionary change. If we reject the Germans' political overtones, there is a parallel between the architects of *Der Blok* and members of the Liverpool school including Velarde and Bernard Miller. Direct associations can only be speculative, but certain works of *Der Blok* members bear a visual resemblance to some Velarde churches, the most obvious being the twin towers topped with copper-clad pyramids of the Gustav Adolf Memorial Church in Nuremberg of 1927–30 by German Bestelmeyer (1874–1942). An architect working in a similar vein was Albert Bosslet (1880–1957), the subject of an article in *Art Notes* in 1939. As the author Joan Morris explains, 'Bosslet prides himself rather in transforming but not severing with past traditions', and the Romanesque arched openings and pyramidal tops to his campaniles find echoes in Velarde's post-war work such as St Alexander's, Bootle, of 1955–7.[14] Velarde himself also wrote for *Art Notes*, which under Reilly's aegis was evacuated to No 5 Abercromby Square, Liverpool, in 1940–1.

Velarde's churches have strong connections with both the German expressionism of Dominikus Böhm and the *Der Blok* group, but in the 1930s his schools were an important part of his work as he established his practice. For these more utilitarian structures Velarde adopted a more popular strand of modernism, the work of Willem Dudok and Erich Mendelsohn. That Mendelsohn was a member of the Der Ring camp rather than *Der Blok* seemed not to have bothered the pragmatic Velarde who, Robert Maxwell recalled, told his students that 'Mendelsohn was OK but Corb was not'.[15] Mendelsohn

Gustav-Adolf Memorial church,
Nurenberg, by German Bestelmeyer

West front of St Alexander's, Bootle
(demolished)

gave a guest lecture at Liverpool University in 1933, which may have influenced Velarde and had considerable impact in the city on young architects such as John Hughes. By then architects were aware of the political situation in Germany, for Sir Giles Scott wrote to Reilly of his shock at how badly Mendelsohn was being treated in his native country and asking if he could sponsor a permanent visa for him.[16]

Within Velarde's school projects of the 1930s, the secondary school at Our Lady of Lourdes, Southport, completed in 1936, was the largest and most architecturally imposing. It is a low, two-storey brick structure, whose very horizontal emphasis is offset by the vertical stair tower that creates a balanced asymmetry very similar to Mendelsohn and Serge Chermayeff's De La Warr Pavilion in Bexhill, built in 1934–5. The internal details of the main stair have a decidedly European modernist feel to them. The De La Warr Pavilion uses a steel frame and exposed concrete details, but Velarde admitted that he was 'rather uncomfortable with concrete and preferring brick'.[17] A more common influence on British modernism in brick was the Netherlands. A visit to Amsterdam in 1924 inspired Liverpool City Council's policy of building flats, and the brick massing and curved staircase towers of Herbert Rowse's rebuilding of the Philharmonic Hall in 1937–9 owes much to the work of Michel de Klerk, Piet Kramer and Willem Dudok. As the city architect for Hilversum, Dudok designed a large number of schools, which were influential on many British municipal architects faced with tight budgets, as well as on Velarde.

Liverpool's post-war European émigrés
During the Second World War an entirely new influence descended on the Liverpool School of Architecture with the creation in 1941 of a Polish School for exiled students. A number of Polish architects stayed in Liverpool after graduation; none were employed by Velarde, although he offered Jerzy Faczynski a job, which he declined in favour of moving to London.[18] Their impact seems to have been more keenly felt by the new generation of post-war students, which included James Stirling, and by the younger members of staff such as Colin Rowe.[19] Faczynski eventually returned to Liverpool to work for Weightman & Bullen, designing the circular St Mary's, Leyland, completed in 1964, before collecting his former mentor's archive with a view to publication, with tragic results: Faczynski's papers, including those from Velarde, were destroyed when his widow's house was cleared in 2006.[20]

In 1950 the prominent Czech modernist Ernst Wiesner joined the teaching staff at Liverpool, having fled his home during the war and briefly working at Oxford. An interesting addition to the international mix, he had converted from Judaism to Catholicism and was friends with Archbishop Heenan,

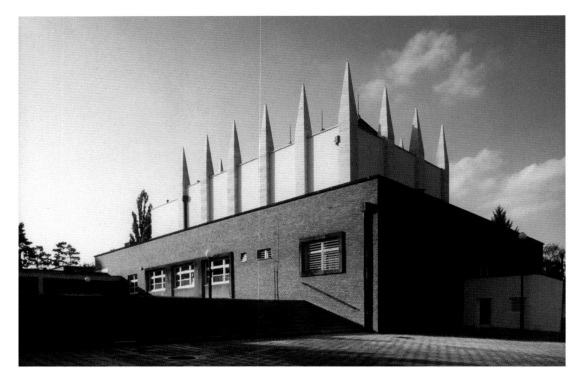

Brno Crematorium 1930, by Ernst Wiesner   Opposite: Holy Cross RC church, Bidston, west front

which helped him gain commissions for St Nicholas's primary and secondary schools adjacent to the cathedral.[21] As a fellow architect and practicing Catholic with connections, he and Velarde had much in common. While most of Wiesner's work in Brno conformed to the functional modernism for which the city is noted, his one major public building, the crematorium built in 1930, is decorated with a series of thin pinnacles in a blind facade of brick and render set high on steps. The pinnacles, or 'mini spires', with their stripped-down, almost child-like geometries, remind us of similar elements in Velarde's Holy Cross, Bidston, of 1957–9.

The Liturgical Movement and changing forms

Strong visual connections were not the only links between Velarde and the work of Dominikus Böhm, Martin Weber and their contemporaries. The Liturgical Movement refocused the worship of Christ on the shared sacrament of the Mass, rather than private devotions to the mediating figures of Mary and the saints. Its origins lie in northern France, when in 1832 Dom Prosper Gueranger refounded the Benedictine Abbey of Solesmes, dedicated

to the study and recovery of early Christian worship. The movement gained impetus in 1909 when, at a conference in Mechelen/Malines in Belgium, Dom Lambert Beauduin articulated a programme whereby the liturgy could once again become central to the lives of the faithful. Using as the basis of his argument Puis x's call for active participation when in 1903 he proclaimed the value of sacred music and the restoration of Gregorian chant in his *motu proprio, Tra le sollecitudini*,[22] Beauduin argued that worship was the action of the people not just the priest.[23]

These ideas were adopted at the abbey of Maria Laach in Germany, which held its own conference in 1914. This was attended by Romano Guardini, a young theologian who sought to reconcile the philosophies of the modern world with the Catholic liturgy, and whose book, *The Spirit of the Liturgy*, in 1918 set out a belief in the universality of the Mass.[24] He was a friend and mentor of the leading church architect Rudolf Schwarz, and there were close links between Maria Laach Abbey and the archdiocese of Cologne where, under Böhm's direction, the Department of Religious Art at the city's School of Applied Art was the centre for the design and decoration of new churches.

As these new interpretations of the liturgy developed, so churches began to be built that explored their spatial implications. The first major example to embody these principles was Notre-Dame du Raincy, built in 1922–3 by Auguste Perret as a war memorial on the site where in 1914 General Maunoury had masterminded the repulse of the German army from the Paris outskirts. As well as demonstrating the qualities of reinforced concrete and modern glass, it offered an uninterrupted view of the altar, with side chapels moved out of this line of sight; the altar was pulled away from the rear wall to create a semblance of a table and the removal of the choir from traditional choir stalls to a rear or side gallery brought the celebrant and congregation closer together. Common features of the movement included low communion rails and wide openings into the sanctuary to maximise sightlines, and at Le Raincy the altar and congregation occupy a single space. The work of Böhm and Schwarz was similarly underpinned by a deep understanding of the relationship between architecture and liturgy.

Velarde and his wife Madge used the summers of the late 1930s to drive through France to Switzerland and Spain. Although he was impressed by Perret's masterpiece and aware of the importance of the Liturgical Movement in the design of contemporary churches, Velarde remained unconvinced about exposed concrete as a finish.[25] He adopted most of the early liturgical developments in his larger churches, beginning at St Monica's, Bootle. This was an early demonstration of these principles in the United Kingdom, although, according to Robert Proctor, 'Before the Second World War, the few British Catholics who noticed the liturgical movement tended to be regarded as eccentric.'[26] At St Monica's, Velarde reduced the side aisles,

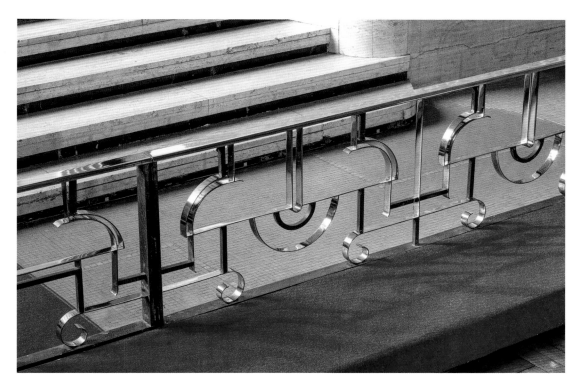

Altar rail in chrome plated steel, St Monica's, Bootle

placed the choir in a raised side gallery and created a large opening into the sanctuary, which is continuous in width and height with the nave. The communion rail was a very low open construction in chromed steel, and he set the altar forward of the rear wall. Velarde repeated the use of a first-floor choir gallery at English Martyrs', Wallasey, in 1952. In his article written in 1953 with his brother, he explained that

> We are agreed today that in the plan of a church the sanctuary should be visible from all points of the building ... The altar is the dramatic focus point of a church interior. The eye should be led up to it, and persuaded to rest in it. Yet the design of altar and sanctuary should not present the eye of the worshipper with too sharp a climax.[27]

Rudolph Schwarz, in his book *The Church Incarnate: The Sacred Function of Christian Architecture*, published in 1958, outlined the development of a church plan which represented the coming together of a group of individuals to form a community for the celebration of the Mass.[28] In an earlier essay, in 1938, he described the experience of standing in a ring:

> In the closed form of the ring the arcing movement which originated it circles incessantly ahead, an inner stream of power which constantly renews and unifies the figure, just as warmly circulating blood sustains and enlivens the human body. The inner stream, dark and hidden, turns the people into a community and unites their bodies into the higher body. This genuine growth befalls the individual who links himself into the common form. The forms of human community are alive. They are exceedingly potent realities which, standing the test of time, prove true. And of them all, the ring is the strongest.[29]

The idea of the circle as the perfect embodiment of the simplest form of celebration, one with the strength to build a community, was a powerful influence on church design. However, it posed some problems. With a centralised plan there is a natural impulse to place the focal point, the altar, in the middle with the congregation all around. Which way, then, should the priest face? Another issue in having people behind the altar is the difficulty of avoiding visual distractions during the Mass. Most 'in-the-round' plans of the 1930s stayed on paper, though an interesting variant was Böhm's St Engelbert's, Cologne-Riehl, of 1928–32. Böhm created a circular nave formed by eight parabolic arches, but he placed the altar in a low, extended sanctuary opposite the entrance. The pews were originally placed linearly, thereby avoiding issues of orientation and background for the priest. More generally, however, Böhm adopted the plan made fashionable by Notre-Dame du Raincy of a linear, rectangular plan, but with a sanctuary within the same volume offering clear sightlines. At his church of Christ the King, Leverkusen, he defined the sanctuary only by two pillars with a set of tall steps ascending to the altar between them.

Awareness of the Liturgical Movement grew among the clergy and their congregations after the Second World War, when the Modern Movement and new construction techniques opened up greater possibilities for spatial innovation. Velarde's position was cautious, calling with his brother for a continuation of aspects of tradition; they argued that conventional rules of architectural composition provided comfort for the congregation and produced more harmonious results, calling modern ornamentation 'trashy, vulgar and cheap – save in terms of money', similar to the arguments he had made against traditional decoration in his lecture back in the 1920s.[30]

Many of Velarde's churches were small and the complexities of side aisles or choir galleries not an issue. However, the larger examples, like St Monica's, Bootle, or English Martyrs', Wallasey, display the principles established in Europe in the inter-war years. He did not progress from this, staying, as he said in his article for the *Clergy Review*, honest to what he saw as fundamental elements. The Liturgical Movement moved on, and by the mid-1950s a new generation of architects were pushing the forms of church design. Churches such as Our Lady of Fatima, Harlow, designed by Gerard Goalen in 1954 (though not built until 1958–60) started to explore cruciform plans, and subsequently circular layouts and fan shapes started to appear. Some of the architects of these churches belonged to the multi-denominational New Churches Research Group, founded in 1957 by Peter Hammond, Robert Maguire and Keith Murray. In 1960 Hammond published *Liturgy and Architecture*, which argued for a modern church architecture based primarily upon the functions of the liturgy. This modern functionalism did not sit well with Velarde, who belonged very definitely to the previous generation. The last church commission he received, St Michael and All Angels, Woodchurch, was built in 1960–4 after his death by a young graduate within his practice, Richard O'Mahony, a member of the New Churches Research Group. This powerful top-lit church was a significant departure.

F X Velarde was a practising Catholic with a desire to craft churches that combined modern statements with the comfort of familiarity for their congregations. He was at the forefront of developments in church design during the 1930s but, by sticking to and refining that style thereafter, appeared increasingly as a glorious eccentric. His work lies somewhere between German expressionism and the English Catholic Byzantine, but always distinctly and ravishingly his own.

3 Churches of the 1920s and 1930s

Velarde began his private practice with a school, and it was school work that paid the bills throughout his career. Yet he made his reputation early with a sophisticated understanding of the problems of modern church design, though his dependence on the patronage of the local Roman Catholic dioceses was also sometimes awkward. Three powerful brick churches designed before the Second World War saw him develop a personal architectural language informed by his training at Liverpool and European travels.

St Matthew's, Clubmoor, 1927–1930

The parish of St Matthew's was established in 1922 to serve the municipal housing estates then being laid out to either side of Queen's Drive, north-east of Liverpool city centre. Queen's Drive has claim to be Britain's first ring road, proposed by the enterprising city engineer John Brodie as early as 1898 and laid out from 1904 onwards.[1] He also assumed responsibility for housing following a financial scandal in the city's Housing Department, until in 1925 pressure from Liverpool's cultural elite, among them Professor Reilly, persuaded him to appoint an architectural assistant. This was Lancelot Keay, elevated to director of housing in 1929 and to city architect in 1938. The new estates were low-density layouts of two-storey 'cottages', short terraces and semi-detached houses erected under the Housing Acts of 1919 and 1924, but lacking sufficient scale to give definition and enclosure to such large roads.[2] So many near-identical houses along near-identical roads in a flat part of Liverpool was disorientating. An attempt at contrast was made with three-storey flats along the nearby Muirhead Avenue, in a watered-down neo-Georgian style by Reilly's protégés Quiggin & Gee, but the area desperately needed some landmarks. With this in mind, a site at the junction of Queen's Drive and Townsend Avenue, a radial road leading to the city centre, was identified for a Roman Catholic church. Another corner site to the east of the ring road was given to Velarde's friend Bernard Miller to produce its Anglican counterpart, St Christopher's, Norris Green, built in 1930–2.

Fr Walter Hothersall was appointed in early 1922 to found a new parish at Clubmoor but died that October, having already been succeeded in post that

Side aisles and internal buttresses, St Monica's, Bootle

September by Fr William Weston. The parishioners first used the loft of a cow byre at the nearby New Hall Farm for services, but in 1922–3 constructed a temporary church on a site adjacent to that earmarked for the permanent church and which later became the parish hall.[3]

Funding for the new church came from an unusual legacy. The architect Matthew Honan (1878–1916), the youngest son of a prominent Catholic family in Liverpool, had trained under Grayson and Ould before attracting the attention of Thomas Whiteside, the first Archbishop of Liverpool. He designed a number of prominent Roman Catholic churches, including St Joseph's, Chorley (1909–10), St Benedict's, Warrington (1911–14), and St Philip Neri, Liverpool (designed by him in 1912 but realised posthumously in a simplified version by M J Worthy and Alfred Rigby). All these churches followed a Byzantine style, and when in 1914 he joined the army, Honan made a will leaving £12,000 towards a new church in the diocese on condition that it adopt this style. He was killed at Beaumont Hamel on the Somme in November 1916. The church at Clubmoor was dedicated to St Matthew in his honour, and memorial masses are still held there each year. By the time work started on the permanent church, interest on the Honan Bequest had seen his donation rise to £14,235.[4]

Looking for a suitable architect, Fr Weston and the Bishop of Liverpool, Robert Dobson, turned to Charles Reilly for advice. Reilly had himself built St Barnabas, Shacklewell, London, in 1909 and extended Holy Trinity, Wavertree, Liverpool, in 1911, but by the 1920s he preferred to pass work to his former students. As a Roman Catholic then working in the practice of Weightman & Bullen favoured by the diocese, Velarde was the perfect candidate for the job, but Fr Weston questioned his youth and inexperience. Velarde personally visited Bishop Dobson to tell him that 'I know I can do it', so securing the commission for Weightman & Bullen's office with himself as the designer.[5] Derek 'Baldy' Bridgwater drew a perspective for exhibition at the Royal Academy and confirmed that St Matthew's was Velarde's own work: 'I worked quite a lot in his office at nights when doing this perspective; and one night we were locked in the building and had, at 3.00 am, to get the Police to let us out. They hardly believed we were Architects working late.'[6] The bishop laid the foundation stone on 19 August 1928 and Archbishop Downey opened the church on 16 March 1930.

St Matthew's has a long nave under a pantiled pitched roof, with a low, narrow flat-roofed north aisle offset by a very tall tower placed asymmetrically between the nave and apsidal sanctuary on the north elevation facing Queens Drive. To the south, a higher aisle containing the Lady Chapel is linked to an adjacent presbytery. The entire composition is faced in brick, with a copper-clad cupola to the tower. The nave walls are subdivided into six bays by

St Matthew's, Clubmoor, photographed by Edward Chambré Hardman upon completion in 1930

small projecting brick pilasters, each bay with pairs of round-headed arched windows, while the north aisle has smaller windows in threes and contains the rather understated entrance porch. This relatively small proportion of window to wall added to the sense of mass, as is typical of the Byzantine style. Nikolas Pevsner was critical of the exterior in general and tower in particular, complaining that 'the top stage with its stubby Romanesque angle columns and its copper cupola is decidedly embarrassing, and the body of the church with small round windows is without distinction'.[7] Nevertheless, the idiosyncratic tower achieves the desired function as a landmark, and the rest of the exterior is a well-mannered and solid exercise in Byzantine church architecture.

Pevsner recognised that the interior revealed Velarde's considerable promise. The first impression is of a single space, set under a shallow arched vault, with a strong focus on the altar framed within a large semicircular sanctuary arch. Such a bold plan is striking for its date, and demonstrates the point made by Velarde in 1953 that in the plan of a church the sanctuary should be visible from all points of the building.[8]

Velarde acknowledged the work of James O'Byrne, a Liverpool architect who designed a nave and chancel as a single space as early as the 1870s.[9] The arch here has the quality of a theatre proscenium, framing and defining the separation of function while allowing a clear view. Yet the sanctuary is only slightly raised: the altar is two steps up from the sanctuary which itself is two steps above the six-bay nave. Below the paired nave windows are semicircular arches into the low side aisles, save on the south side where two arches combine to make a higher arched opening into the Lady Chapel, subsequently closed off. Round arches provide a recurring motif, from the arcades and windows to the ends of the long bench pews; the woodwork was by William Burden. The choir occupied a gallery over the low west end and baptistery.

Within the sanctuary the altar sits beneath a ciborium, its round-arched dome supported on four gently Solomonic columns all in gold, with some green to the base and canopy. Velarde wrote in 1953 that the ciborium,

Nave, St Matthew's, Clubmoor, Liverpool

baldacchino or tester 'gives not only dignity to an altar, but also a certain precious and splendid quality, and with a little ingenuity in the use of material can be produced at a very moderate cost'.[10] St Matthew's shows his fondness for gold, and his enjoyment of its opulence when set against bare brickwork.[11] He also loved angels and would use them as a decorative symbol throughout his life, from embellishments to altars, window mullions for schools, and for Christmas cards. At St Matthew's, the stone altar is picked out in gold and blue, and decorated with three panels depicting angels and fish carved in bas relief by Herbert Tyson Smith. When first completed, the sanctuary was finished in bare common brick, as the nave still is, which contrasted powerfully with the ornate altar, as with Bentley's work at Westminster Cathedral so admired by Reilly. Appropriately, it was in this form that the building was illustrated in 1932 in a book celebrating Reilly's retirement from the school of architecture.[12] However, as in the chapels at Westminster, ornate mosaics were later added to the sanctuary walls, providing richness perhaps at the expense of power. The Stations of the Cross were also carved by Tyson Smith to Velarde's designs and are another fine exercise in bas relief.

Christmas card design
by Velarde

Stations of the Cross by Herbert Tyson Smith to designs by Velarde, St Matthew's, Clubmoor
Opposite: Ciborium and high altar with carvings by Herbert Tyson Smith, St Matthew's, Clubmoor

The church has been little altered since its completion in 1930; the nave and sanctuary were sufficiently open and connected that reordering following the Second Vatican Council was not considered necessary. Space might also have been a consideration, for there was a large congregation in the parish into the 1960s. Externally the form is unaltered, although maintenance is a problem for what is now a small parish; Historic England have identified that the roofs need renewing and have placed St Matthew's on its Heritage at Risk list. The one change has been to the Lady Chapel, finished in the same brickwork as the main church. It was separated to form a self-contained space for everyday events and children's services in the early 1990s, but still has an altar, set up two steps in a shallow apse and with a gilded reredos. A corridor links it to the presbytery.

This is a complete example of Velarde's early work, a building much loved and respected by its congregation. It shows his distinctive style in formation, with flashes of his mature language in its fixtures and use of colour, and particularly in the collaboration with Tyson Smith.

St Gabriel's, Brownhill Drive, Blackburn, 1932–1933

Velarde's only Anglican church, St Gabriel's was built in the centre of a new municipal housing estate on the northern outskirts of Blackburn. The cost of £15,000 was largely raised by the parishioners, most of whom were cotton weavers and many of whom were out of work. They formed an ambitious building committee determined to erect a church that was modern in spirit as well as in materials, and invited Professor Reilly to give a slide lecture on recent churches in England and on the Continent. He proposed that the committee approach Velarde but, as the latter's son Giles recalled, the evangelical Revd Albert Smith and his congregation were so wary of appointing a young Roman Catholic that Reilly suggested that they also approach Bernard Miller and offered to act as an arbitrator. Though the resulting scheme was initially jointly attributed, Miller insisted that the entire credit for the design should go to his friend.[13] With a brief to be wholly modern, the design shows the influence of Velarde's travels through Germany. 'That it is a credit and a definite contribution to the architecture of our own time all who have seen it will agree', was the commendation of the *Manchester Guardian*.[14]

Externally, St Gabriel's was a powerful composition of interlocking brick boxes, accentuated by setting the steeply pitched black-tiled nave roof behind parapets. The stepped forms have something of Paul Bonatz's Stuttgart Railway Station, and still more of the brick churches built across the Rhineland around 1930. The monolithic quality is enhanced by the use of two-inch orange Stamford bricks, with wide joints in a coarse lime mortar. Velarde later wrote that

Correctly handled, even the simplest materials can give a dignified result ... As brick is commonly used, it is important not only to choose a good brick but to use also suitably coloured mortar. Recall that mortar constitutes about thirty per cent of the surface of brick building, so that a mistake here is fatal. Pure cement mortar should be avoided, and those also that are made from crushed cinders instead of sand.[15]

The windows of the five-bay nave, like those at St Matthew's, are set against a mass of this plain brickwork and paired under semicircular heads, but here they are stretched vertically until they are little more than slender slots with strainer arches above, giving a greater impression of solidarity. The side aisles have also been taken upwards so that they almost reach the top of the nave. This places the windows in the aisles rather than the nave, giving as subtle a penetration of natural light into the body of the church as Ivar Tengbom achieved at the Högalid Church in Stockholm. Above the arcades are five very small square windows rather than a continuous clerestory to lighten the mass. The chancel was expressed by a greater height, where a cluster of four narrow windows shone light directly on to the choir, here placed in their traditional location between the nave and the sanctuary. Instead of the apse found at St Matthew's, there are three diminishing brick rectangles untroubled by windows.

A squat rectangular tower containing the entrance rises from the south-west corner. This went through several versions, at first incorporating tall round-headed stepped openings as at Böhm's Christ the King, Leverkusen, and St Kamillus, Mönchengladbach, but this device was dropped from the final scheme in favour of a modest doorway set below another pair of stretched windows and two lines of round-headed belfry openings. The bulky west end has four more slot windows in an otherwise blind elevation; the doorway in the tower is the only entrance. The conventional Byzantine exterior of St Matthew's has gone, save for the pairing of the round-headed windows; instead there is a confident interpretation of German expressionism.

The entrance originally led into a wonderfully polished steel and glass lobby that would not have looked out of place in an Art Deco hotel. Otherwise St Gabriel's forsook the decorative richness of St Matthew's in favour of greater spatial inventiveness. Evocative black and white photographs, taken upon completion by Velarde's friend Edward Chambré Hardman, provide the best impression of the intended lighting effects. Their impact is accentuated by the rendering of the internal walls in rough sand plaster, painted beige, which eliminated the tectonic qualities of the brick exterior in favour of texture, a heightened geometry and contrasts between light and shadow. This was particularly effective in the nave, where the windows were concealed by internal buttresses, linked to form a

St Gabriel's, Blackburn, nearing completion, photographed by Edward Chambré Hardman in 1933

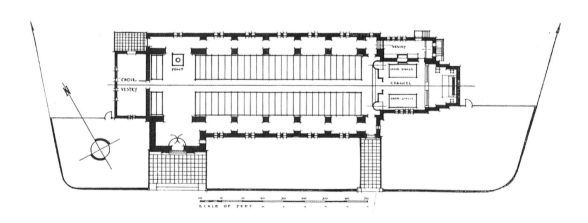

St Gabriel's, Blackburn, plan

View towards the sanctuary, St Gabriel's, Blackburn, photographed by Edward Chambré Hardman in 1933

View of the nave, St Gabriel's, Blackburn, photographed by Edward Chambré Hardman in 1933

round-arched arcade and pierced to allow a passage aisle. The barrel vault of the nave springs directly from the arcade without even a string course and is finished in the same plaster, adding to the monumental effect. Velarde's experiments in bold colour were restricted to the heavy, close-centred downstand beams of the narthex and chancel, and to the fittings.

Many of the furnishings were also more muted than those at St Matthew's, with the nave floors and pews in waxed oak and the floor and dado of the chancel finished in travertine marble. Pulpit and lectern complemented each other, resembling pairs of ambos in a Catholic church, and terminated a low screen; all were made of travertine. Chromed steel on the reredos, in the light fittings and framing the entrance lobby provided a sparkle among the beige. The door and window frames had the strong colours later favoured by Velarde, here a bright peacock blue with gold highlights, while the reredos featured two shades of brilliant red. The original glass was mainly clear with small random insets in deep blue, to which Brian Clarke added a baptistery window in 1977.

The overall effect was of a powerful space carved from a single material, the diminishing arches of the chancel and altar adding an Art Deco feel accented by decorative details in the doors and windows. Among the most modern churches of its day, as the *Manchester Guardian* noted, it 'proves to

Decoesque door detail, St Gabriel's, Blackburn

anyone who may have doubted the possibility that a very worshipful and reverent structure can be built today on entirely modern lines by the right artist'.[16] Julian Leathart considered that 'The innate qualities of restraint and simplicity so apparent in the treatment of the form of this church have a spirituality at once appropriate and inspiring. There is a Puritanical severity of line and massing which indicates the development of the plan-form to its logical conclusion by controlled expression without striving for objective architectural effect.'[17] J P Alcock considered that 'In the finely massed exterior of St Gabriel's, Blackburn, there is a sense of power and decision. It is hard, looking at this building, to realize that the architect was bound by such conditions as economy, byelaws and the necessity of keeping out the weather.'[18] Edward Maufe and Charles Reilly also gave positive reviews.[19]

Sadly, this church has been much altered, and is in a poor condition due to water ingress and settlement. Problems were first recognised in 1956, and in 1970–1 Grimshaw & Townsend removed the parapets and continued the nave roof to conventional projecting eaves with downpipes (features which Velarde would have hated), visually crushing the body of the church while spoiling the formal connection between the external massing and internal spatial composition. The tower and chancel were lowered and over-clad in brown metal panels, which have also been applied to the vestry and west end. Yet despite these interventions the building's original elegance can still be discerned. More seriously, a number of structural cracks have appeared in the brickwork, probably as a result of the church being built upon landfill, and there must be concern for the long-term future of the building, for services are now held only in the church hall. The most powerful valedictory came from Gavin Stamp:

> The blocky brick exterior was reminiscent of a power station or, perhaps, of the Mersey Tunnel ventilating shafts, while the Moderne plastered interior was given interest by decorative light fittings and an amazing chromium reredos. Unfortunately as the structure began to leak, permission was given ... to rebuild the upper parts of the building, replace the ceiling vault and, for no good reason, to remove Velarde's chromium reredos. This is the sort of treatment which would no longer be tolerated for a good Georgian or Victorian church and must not be allowed to happen again to the best interwar churches.[20]

St Monica's, Bootle, 1933–1936

The last of Velarde's inter-war churches, and the most highly regarded, Pevsner described St Monica's as 'an epoch-making church for England'.[21] Now listed grade I, it is a total work of architecture, thanks not only to its European influences but to the collaborations between Velarde and his favourite artists. Large and well maintained, with few alterations, it achieves the effect he intended for his churches, as noted in his obituary, to 'brighten the drab parts in which they are to be found'.[22]

A small resort town north of Liverpool, Bootle expanded rapidly in the late 19th century with the arrival of the railway and the extension of docks along the Mersey estuary. The Roman Catholic population grew accordingly. In 1922 Fr Benedict Cain established the mission of St Monica in a large Victorian house on Breeze Hill next to the Anglican parish church, before acquiring a site at Fernhill close to the Liverpool boundary, where Lord Derby had gifted land for a park in 1895.[23] A temporary church opened in 1923, but as new housing estates were built and the parish grew, it rapidly became too small. A fundraising scheme encouraged parishioners to 'buy a brick'; in return they were given a plan of the church showing the location of their purchases.

The building of the permanent church was taken up by a new parish priest, Dr John Foley. The site at the north-east corner of Derby Park is bounded by the junction of Fernhill and Earl Roads, constrained by these two streets and existing housing to the north and west. The limited opportunity to expand posed design problems for Velarde, leading to slightly fractious letters between him, Foley and the archdiocese concerning the size of the congregation that could be accommodated before he produced a final design seating 500 souls.[24] The archdiocese had wanted 800.[25] On 4 May 1935, Archbishop Downey laid the foundation stone, returning on 4 October 1936 for the opening ceremony. The church cost £18,000, which considering its size and the quality of its craftsmanship represented good value.

For Velarde, this commission followed the protracted convalescence from his car crash in 1932, which gave him time to reflect on the buildings he had seen on his Rhineland tour and to draw. Böhm's influence was at its greatest in the facade to St Monica's. There are also references to Martin Weber's Holy Cross (Heilig-Kreuz-Kirche), Frankfurt, of 1928–9, which he had photographed extensively. As *Building* commented, 'the mass of St Monica's Church, although possessed of all the gracious restfulness of the smaller village churches of the past, will always remain a church that is instinctively with the best traditions of the 20th-century vernacular'.[26]

Externally, St Monica's is faced in two-inch brownish grey Hadley bricks from Shropshire, set in half-inch lime mortar joints coloured with red Parbold sand. The similarity in tone between the bricks and joints gave a monolithic appearance that has sadly been lost with later repointing in a lighter mortar.

St Monica's was Velarde's first use of a dominant mass of masonry in lieu of a tower or campanile, commanding the corner site and anchoring the building. It is not strictly a *Westwerk*, for the church faces east rather

St Monica's, Bootle, view towards east (liturgical west) end

than west. It is dominated by three large Portland stone angels, carved by Herbert Tyson Smith, raised over tall, round-headed windows set in blocks of two by four, an expression of the English perpendicular tradition at its most minimal. The body of the church has six bays, with arrays of windows set into the high side aisles, as at St Gabriel's, above which square flying buttresses connect to the only slightly higher nave, where very small, unadorned pairs of windows form a clerestory. The mass of the nave continues eastwards to form the sanctuary, which is without an apse. A single large window on the south elevation, set above a side chapel, illuminates the sanctuary; that on the north side is concealed behind a choir gallery. Velarde explained that 'it is attractive to have south and south-west sunlight streaming into the sanctuary on the gospel side. This means that the morning Mass congregation will suffer no inconvenience, while during

St Monica's, Bootle, viewed across Derby Park, photographed by Edward Chambré Hardman in 1936

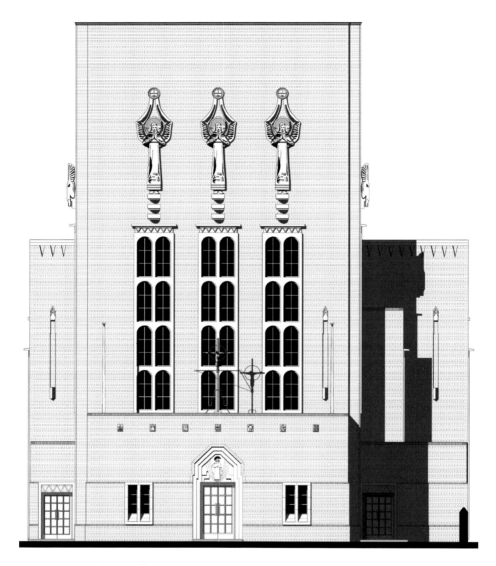

St Monica's, Bootle, east (liturgical west) elevation drawn by Isaac Crompton

the rest of the day the building will be suffused with warm sunlight.' He advised against a window at the back of the sanctuary 'because at its best the brightness of the light distracts attention from the altar, and at the worst it almost blinds those kneeling in the front and centre of the church.'[27]

Charles Reilly described the interior as displaying a 'quality of the imagination ... which few recent churches anywhere can equal'. He drew parallels

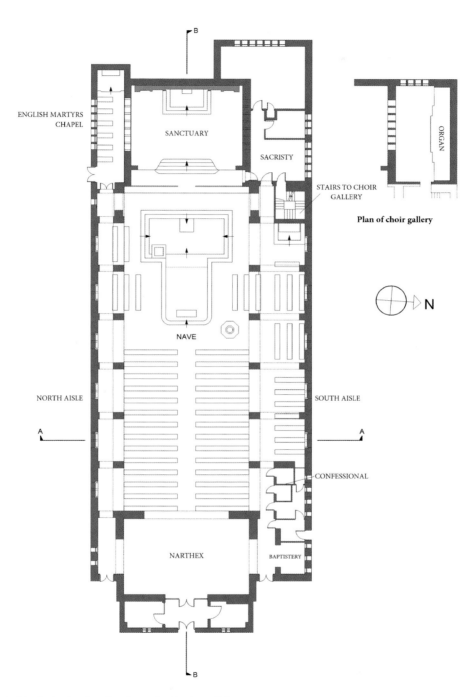

ENGLISH MARTYRS CHAPEL

SANCTUARY

SACRISTY

STAIRS TO CHOIR GALLERY

ORGAN

Plan of choir gallery

N

NAVE

NORTH AISLE

SOUTH AISLE

A

A

CONFESSIONAL

NARTHEX

BAPTISTERY

St Monica's, Bootle, plan drawn by Matthew Usher

St Monica's, Bootle, screen to choir gallery, under construction

with the Högalid Church in its detailing, although the main similarity, as
at St Gabriel's, is in the composition of the passage aisles as tall arcades
of internal buttresses punctured with arches at low level.[28] The nave
and sanctuary are set under an almost continuous pitched roof in green-
grey pantiles. The creation of the nave and sanctuary as an almost single
space is an interesting development and is still more striking internally,
where it resembles earlier works by Sir Giles Scott and reflects the spirit of
the Liturgical Movement. The walls and arcades are finished in exposed
brown brick, and contrast with a highly decorated reredos and canopy in
the sanctuary. Elevating the choir into a gallery on the north side of the
sanctuary over the sacristy reduced the physical separation between the
priest and congregation. Velarde's rationale was that the choir was there 'to

lead the congregation and encourage it, but not to do its work'.[29] He had first proposed placing the choir in a west-end gallery, and the suggestion to place it to the side of the sanctuary came from Dr Foley. Velarde commented that 'This in many ways is a good position for a choir, but I should point out that it will rob the sanctuary of side light and the sacristies of top light'.[30] The Builder was most impressed, commenting that the innovation 'has released the church from a very ugly feature which usually cramps the west end and blocks the main window with its organ and equipment'.[31] It is framed internally with a screen of unglazed 'windows' matching those on the south elevation. The abstraction of this screen, uncompromised by window frames, achieves an Italian rationalist feel, akin to a painting by Giorgio de Chirico (1888–1978).

There are only five steps up to the altar and a very light communion rail to set the priest apart from his congregation, while the flat ceiling is almost uninterrupted. Janet Gnosspelius reported that Velarde was worried that churches were bad for speech, so was careful about his ceiling shapes and came to avoid barrel vaults, preferring stilted roof trusses with soft celotex ceiling board as a sound absorbent.[32] Alcock noted that 'the necessity of an acoustic surface in the ceiling has been so handled as to become a positive gain in the decorative scheme'.[33]

The fittings at St Monica's are very fine and, apart from some reordering by Richard O'Mahony in 1986, are original. Every detail was considered, designed and drawn by Velarde, including the water stoops in the shape of Ionic capitals, the bentwood sanctuary chairs with their scrolled arms, the glass and chrome light fittings (now lost), the Art Deco lectern, and the mosaic floors of the baptistery and English Martyrs' chapel. The most prominent internal features are the richly decorated altar (by Tyson Smith), the canopy and the reredos, the latter disliked by Pevsner, who noted that 'it is a great pity that the altar wall is so prettified'. The reredos, occupying the entire (liturgical) east wall, has a chequerboard pattern of slightly raised rectangles flanked towards the edges with slender stylised Ionic pilasters, and is decorated with six ascending angels. These figures, carved by W L Stevenson, are to designs by Velarde. Floating above the altar is a rectangular canopy slightly arched in the middle, again with a geometric pattern but this time of brightly coloured squares, held at the four corners by stars and scrolls; the actual support is from chains decorated with crosses hung from the ceiling. The angels, canopy and pilasters are picked out in gold, set against a white background. The pale colour palette of the sanctuary, flooded with light from the south window, contrasts dramatically with the otherwise dark brick interior, instantly establishing this as the focal point of the church. Stevenson was also responsible for the fine Stations

Sanctuary and altar, St Monica's, Bootle, photographed by Edward Chambré Hardman, 1936

of the Cross, in the style established by Eric Gill, which are located on each brick pier along the nave. The slender and lightweight communion rail, barely there at all, is in an Art Deco pattern of semicircles and flat bars, all finished in chrome, a very playful treatment of this ceremonially important feature that perhaps reflects Velarde's sense of humour. When asked why he incorporated irregular and asymmetrical compositions into his churches, he replied that he thought 'it would make God laugh'.[34]

St Monica's altar, canopy and reredos

Detail to edge of altar canopy, St Monica's, Bootle

The aisle on the north side (liturgical south) is just wide enough to incorporate a Lady Chapel, while the narrower one opposite terminates in a long, thin chapel dedicated to the English Martyrs where a triptych depicting St Thomas More, St John Fisher and colleagues is signed 'G W' and dated 1938. The chrome finish, first employed by Velarde in the entrance lobby at St Gabriel's, is also used for the gates to the English Martyrs' chapel and even on the mantels over the radiators. These were the work of George Burden, described as 'in a small way of business, who only a few years ago specialised in gas meters'. His brother William produced all the woodwork, including the reredos as well as all the furniture, showing how Velarde worked with a close-knit yet skilled team.[35] The drawings in silver on the otherwise plain glass of the sanctuary windows were by Marjorie Brooks (Mrs W G Holford), a Rome scholar in decorative painting and another close family friend. Here she drew figures of saints directly on to the surface of the glass, sealed by a secondary layer of glass internally for protection.

O'Mahony's reordering was sensitive. By moving the altar on to a new low platform at the (liturgical) east end of the nave, it was possible to leave the original altar and communion rail in place, retaining the essence of the sanctuary design. The reorientation of some of the pews creates a slightly awkward relationship with the aisles and the modern red carpet is very definitely not a Velarde colour, but otherwise St Monica's remains much as intended, described by the *Architect and Building News* as having 'a nave of majestic proportions and immense romantic appeal'.[36]

4 Schools and housing

Commissions for new churches during the 1930s arrived erratically, and relying on them to maintain an architectural practice was financially challenging. Fortunately for Velarde, the Roman Catholic Church was also very active in the construction of schools. The Education Act of 1902 had provided state funding for Roman Catholic schools in England and Wales, while the Act of 1918 had raised the leaving age to 14, leading to the building of more senior elementary and secondary schools.[1] A series of six committees chaired by Henry Hadow, vice-chancellor of Sheffield University, between 1920 and 1933 investigated a range of education issues from nursery schools to the provision of books. One enduring legacy was the division of state education between primary and secondary schools at age 11, another was the pressure exerted on schools administered by the Anglican and Roman Catholic churches to improve their buildings and curricula. Initial resistance from the churches gave way in the face of a greater concern at the loss of pupils to more modern state schools, particularly in the larger urban areas.[2]

Our Lady of Lourdes RC Primary and Secondary Schools, Grantham Road, Birkdale, 1930–1942

The Roman Catholic primary school of Our Lady of Lourdes in Birkdale, Southport, was commissioned in 1930 in part as a response to these educational developments. It received positive reviews upon its completion in 1936, not least from the *Architectural Review*: 'Among the forbidding generality of English school buildings this new one, the elementary school of Our Lady of Lourdes at Southport, stands out as one that achieves a considerable step in the proper direction, towards simplicity of outline and clarity of conception.'[3] An austere, flat-roofed modern building in brick, the overall horizontal composition is emphasised by glazing bars that contrast with the more traditionally proportioned vertical window openings. Here is a building at a point of transition in architectural language and struggling to reconcile two styles. The plan is a straightforward single-banked corridor with classrooms to the south,

Stair tower, Our Lady of Lourdes RC Secondary School, Southport, photographed shortly after completion in 1942

which is repeated on its two floors. For reasons of economy (the final cost was just £11,000) and the need for large, repetitive spans, Velarde did not adopt his favoured load-bearing masonry but turned to a concrete frame, which he clad in two-inch brick with flush mortar joints. He used timber for the windows, fearing that the maritime air would corrode steel.[4]

One distinctive Velarde feature is an elaborate porch at the slightly projecting main entrance. There are carvings of St Francis on one side and St George and the dragon on the other, undertaken by Herbert Tyson Smith, who also provided two flanking angels and a panel depicting Our Lady giving blessing to a devotee. One of the angels was a surplus carving from his work for Velarde at St Monica's, Bootle.[5]

The scheme originally included a small temporary chapel at the centre where the corridor formed a dogleg. This was a simple, rectangular rendered building with a pitched tiled roof, which served the parish until a permanent church by L A G Prichard was completed in 1956. Inside, the plain walls

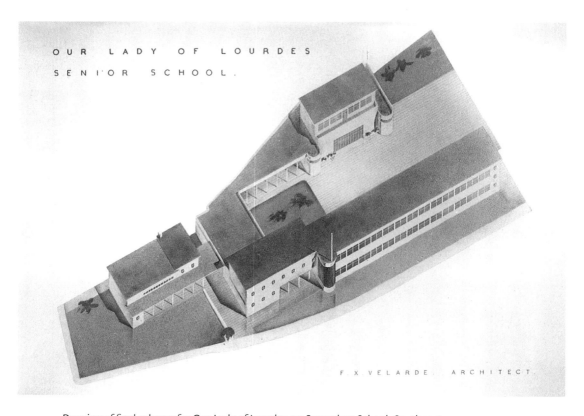

Drawing of final scheme for Our Lady of Lourdes RC Secondary School, Southport

Temporary chapel, Our Lady of Lourdes RC elementary school, which functioned as the parish church until 1956 when it was converted to the school hall

of painted brickwork were offset by a stylised altar, solid communion rail and triptych, all featuring the semicircular motif Velarde had used at St Matthew's. The altar was dressed with a full set of Velarde's silver and gilt candlesticks and a gilt tabernacle. The chapel is now the school hall and no trace remains of the fittings.

The Hadow reports also led to the 1936 Education Act, which raised the school leaving age to 15, a move frustrated only by the outbreak of the Second World War.[6] Critical to the implementation of the Act was the provision of grants to the denominational schools, covering between 50 and 70 per cent of their construction costs, in exchange for the transfer of their management to the local education authorities. This prompted proposals by the Church of England for 230 new schools, and the Roman Catholic Church for 289 across England and Wales.[7] They included a secondary school by Velarde at Southport, squeezed alongside his earlier school on the wedge-shaped site. Begun in 1937, it finally opened in 1942, construction having slowed with the outbreak of war. By this time pupil numbers had been swelled by evacuees

Our Lady of Lourdes RC Secondary School front elevation; note changes from final
scheme drawing

from Liverpool and the primary school, doubling up for both ages, had
become extremely overcrowded.[8]

Located adjacent to and connected with the primary school, the overall
massing maintained a consistent building line and eaves height to the main
elevation facing Grantham Road. This is where the similarities end. The
secondary school has a far more modernist and European feel, with the main
classroom block glazed with two bands of horizontal steel-framed windows.
This strong horizontal emphasis is terminated by a taller stair tower with a
semicircular prow, which Velarde fully glazed using narrow vertical timber
frames. The composition begs comparisons with the schools of Willem
Dudok or Erich Mendelsohn's De La Warr Pavilion at Bexhill.[9] Velarde had
entered the competition for Bexhill, but his entry was unplaced. Sadly, the
timber and steel windows have all been replaced in uPVC, in the case of the
stair tower as recently as 2018, after 71 years of resistance to the sea air. To
the left of the stair tower, a four bay brick block raised on concrete columns
creating an open undercroft that leads into the courtyard playground. Single-
storey buildings flank the courtyard on two sides, where open-sided arcades
formed by concrete columns lead to the gymnasium block that terminates
the composition. This is the largest internal space, a double-height sports

Our Lady of Lourdes RC Secondary School, Southport, gymnasium block

hall lit by clerestory windows, flanked by a pair of apsidal changing blocks. Pevsner noted that it was 'very modern for its date'.[10]

As at the primary school, Velarde adopted a concrete frame, this time expressing the roof slab with a projecting eaves that further emphasises the horizontal flow of the facade. The bricks are matched between the two buildings, which provides some coherence to their contrasting articulations. A new and important Velarde detail appears for the first time on this project, the carved angel as a mullion. Within both horizontal bands, each window is separated by an angel, in material matching the window sill and head. First in stone and later in cast concrete, angels and sometimes doves would appear in almost all Velarde's subsequent buildings, whether churches or schools.

Scalby Senior School, Fieldstead Crescent, Scalby, Scarborough, North Yorkshire

In October 1936 the RIBA *Journal* commented that 'From time to time the profession's conscience turns to concentrate on some national architectural problem. At one time it will be housing, at another the preservation of some monument or a problem of town and country planning. Now it is school building.'[11] Sensing this mood, the *News Chronicle* newspaper

79

organised a competition in 1937 for an ideal secondary school, which was won by Denis Clarke Hall. A timely exhibition followed at the Royal Institute of British Architects, which was devoted to new European school architecture and included Velarde's work at Southport. These schemes were seen by Frank Barraclough, the progressive if hard-headed chief education officer for the North Riding of Yorkshire, who commissioned both Clarke Hall and Velarde to design schools. Velarde's school at Scalby, Scarborough, completed in 1942, was unique in his oeuvre in not being for the Roman Catholic Church.

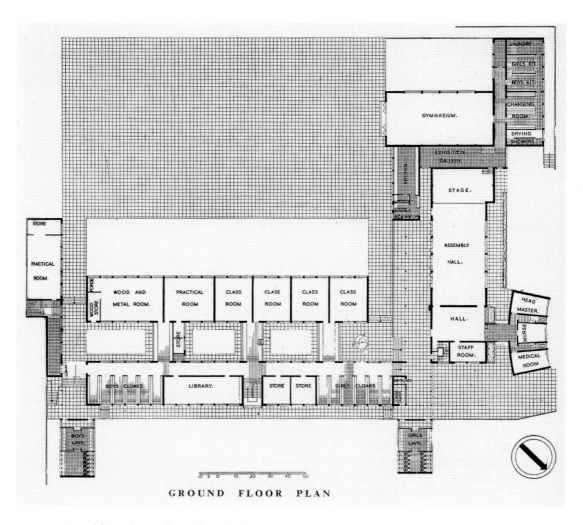

Ground floor plan, Scalby Senior School

Scalby Senior School, assembly block, photographed upon completion in 1942

Designed to accommodate 320 boys and girls on a flat site in the middle of a new housing estate, Scalby School comprises an L-shaped configuration of blocks, mostly of two storeys. Its innovative plan sets the ground-floor classrooms down short spur corridors to permit natural light and ventilation on two sides, a development of the courtyard plan adopted by Clarke Hall at Richmond which was noted by the *Architects' Journal*.[12] This separation also mitigated noise from the main corridor. Thanks to its extensive publication, Velarde's school may have influenced better-known schools by Yorke, Rosenberg and Mardall in Stevenage and Poplar that employed similar spurs.[13] Yet surprisingly, when Velarde heard Clarke Hall lecture at a London conference on schools in 1947, he described him as 'uninteresting'.[14]

The assembly hall and gymnasium formed the short leg of the L at one end of the classroom block, to which a covered external arcade provided

Scalby Senior School, classroom interior showing double aspect to allow greater light and ventilation, photographed in 1942

a link as at Our Lady of Lourdes Secondary School. Now much extended, Scalby maintained the concern for economy in school design.[15] Its concrete frame was infilled in brick with horizontal bands of glazing, within which the windows were approximately square, separated by mullions of cast artificial stone. The angels found at Our Lady of Lourdes were substituted by secular Ionic pilasters. The flat roof was intended as a terrace for the upper-storey classrooms, though it is not known if this was ever used. The building opened in 1942, the same year as Our Lady of Lourdes Secondary School, and both were fully reviewed and models exhibited. However, post-war austerity meant that there was little opportunity to capitalise on this publicity.

The Second World War and Velarde's extreme ill health in 1940 made for an interregnum in his work. The family had to rely upon income from his part-time teaching at the University of Liverpool and Madge's role as a military driver. Any work was produced by Velarde unaided. But as the national economy began to revive in 1945, he started to look for opportunities in new fields, including housing at Bilston, near Wolverhampton, under the aegis of Professor Reilly. Despite the close relationship between

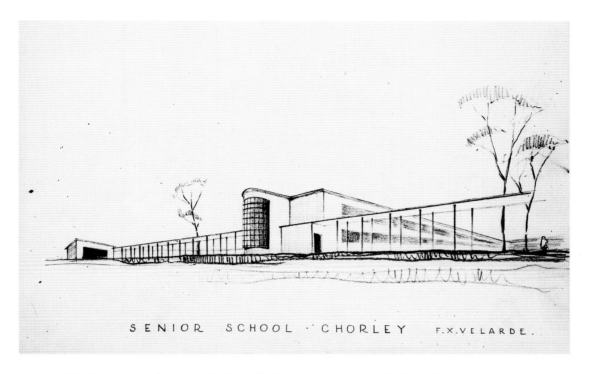

SENIOR SCHOOL · CHORLEY   F.X.VELARDE.

Velarde's drawing of a proposed scheme for Chorley RC Secondary Girls' School, 1945

the departments of Civic Design and Architecture at Liverpool University, Velarde had shown no interest in town planning until he was invited to enter a competition for a Catholic university, with housing and a cinema, in the small town of Oye in central Nigeria.

Instead Velarde focused on a new wave of rather prosaic projects, among them a series of schools in Huyton that included a temporary infants' school composed of wartime military huts.[16] A more ambitious project at Chorley came to nothing, as did attempts to secure more work from the North Riding County Council, and Velarde's attention switched back to churches.[17] The practice did undertake numerous school projects to meet the demands of the 1944 Education Act, mainly for the Liverpool Archdiocese, including additions to St Mary's College, Crosby, and new schools such as St Alphonsus Primary School (rebuilt after war damage), St Aloysius Primary School at Roby, and St Columba's Schools, Huyton.[18] In Cheshire he was commissioned to design Holy Cross School at Bidston and St Bede's Secondary Modern School, Handbridge, Chester (completed in 1953), in addition to smaller works for the Diocese of Shrewsbury.

Hall Green Estate, Bilston, 1946–1947

The origins of Velarde's involvement in the Hall Green housing estate lay in Charles Reilly's attempts to realise his ideas for a new model of social housing based around what became known as 'Reilly Greens'. They can be traced back to Reilly's Roscoe lecture, 'The body of the town', in 1934; an article in 1941, 'The suburbs we should build'; and his attack on the 1942 Royal Academy Plan for London.[19] Never a fan of the conventional cottage suburb, his writings in the early 1940s saw him come to accept low-rise housing but to adopt a communal approach. He recognised that most estates comprised pairs of semi-detached houses that deliberately faced away from each other along curving roads, and instead advocated the creation of small communities of between 500 and 1,000 people based around shared green spaces containing social facilities.[20] The concept had parallels with Thomas Sharp's writings from the 1930s on community planning.[21]

In 1944 there appeared an opportunity to apply these principles when Reilly was appointed planning consultant for the County Borough of Birkenhead. The borough engineer, Bertram Robinson, had prepared a design for a new suburb on 350 acres of countryside at Woodchurch, one of the last true villages in the central Wirral, which Reilly saw by chance on one of his visits to the council. This was a conventional affair, exactly the kind of development that Reilly railed against in his articles. Battle lines formed. Two opposing schemes, one conventional by the engineer and the other by Reilly based around village greens clustered like 'the petals of a flower' were pitted against each other in the local and national press, including *Picture Post* and the *Architects' Journal*. The discussion within the local authority split along party lines, with the Conservatives (the majority party) supporting Robinson and Labour supporting Reilly. The 'Battle of Birkenhead' was lost by Reilly on a political vote, but was not won by Robinson.[22] The eventual scheme was a compromise, with Herbert Rowse appointed to design a new layout. As Rowse was another of Reilly's former students, a version of the professor's plan might have been expected, but the result was more conventional, its small greens dominated by three grand Beaux-Arts avenues radiating from the old parish church.

Velarde himself was initially critical of Reilly's enthusiasm, complaining how, on seeing the professor in July 1945, 'CHR looked far from well but still pursing all sorts of trivialities and intriguing, for what he thinks fame, when everyone behind his back is thinking he has latterly betrayed the cause of architecture especially in his dealings with the Woodchurch housing estate near Birkenhead ... when he should be at home resting and reflecting on the great realities'. But soon Velarde found himself drawn into Reilly's last great campaign at Bilston in Staffordshire.

Bilston was one of the oldest industrial centres in the Black Country. Its ambitious town clerk, Vivian Williams, read about the Battle of Birkenhead and invited Reilly to realise his vision as part of his slum clearance programme. Despite his advanced age and declining health, Reilly embraced the project energetically, bringing in his favourite ex-students, including Derek Bridgwater, William Crabtree and Bernard Miller as well as Velarde to build under his supervision. Janet Gnosspelius remembered that the experience 'showed Mr Velarde working under the direction of a senior architect and from time to time deferring to his judgement', the only time this happened after he left Weightman & Bullen.[23] Such was the scale of the work that Velarde brought in his university assistant, G G Dobson, as a junior partner.[24] The working method between Reilly and Velarde was

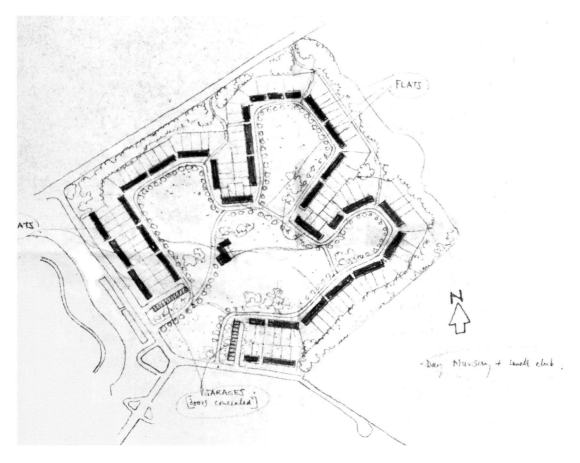

William Crabtree's plan for a 'Reilly Green' housing scheme at Bradley Lane South, Bilston, 1947

85

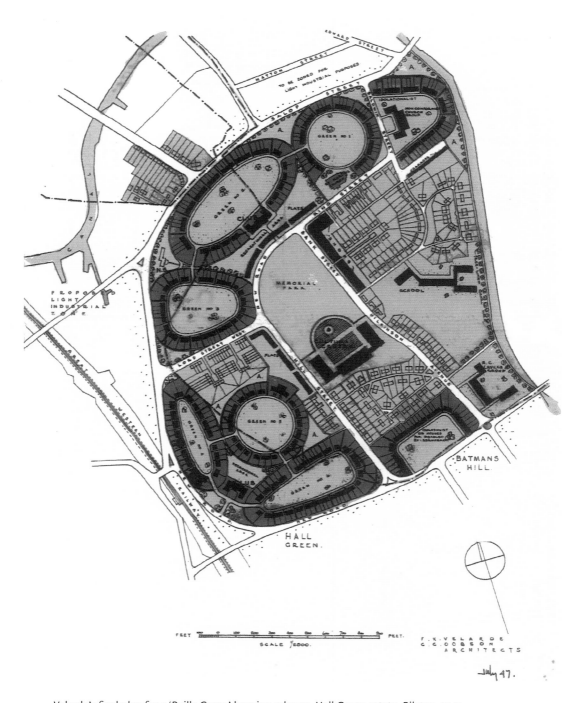

Velarde's final plan for a 'Reilly Green' housing scheme, Hall Green estate, Bilston, 1947

akin to that of master and student: Reilly would make a suggestion, Velarde would draw a plan and send it to Reilly for comment, then after a couple of tweaks the client and Reilly would both be sent a final proposal. There seem to have been several delays in obtaining accurate survey information from the borough engineer, leading Velarde to complain bitterly to Reilly about abortive work based on poor surveys; the engineers for their part denied any errors. The continuous toing and froing slowed the project at a critical juncture, since Reilly was by now seriously ill and in a nursing home. The Bradley Lane North scheme also ran into delays because Bernard Miller was short of staff and busy with churches elsewhere.

By early 1948 Reilly was too ill to continue, and he died on 2 February 1948. With his passing the project lost all momentum, despite the enthusiasm of Williams's successor, confusingly also called Williams. Velarde focused on the competition for a Catholic University in Nigeria and the detailed design of Our Lady of Pity, Greasby, and appears to have had no more involvement after the delivery of the final report and plan. None of the Bilston schemes progressed after Reilly's death, save for watered-down versions of Ella Briggs's and William Crabtree's housing at Stowlawn. A M Williams could secure government funding for only 20 houses at Bradley, and Velarde's scheme of six Reilly Greens remained unbuilt. Vivian Williams had moved on to the neighbouring borough of Dudley in April 1946, where Bridgwater and Shepheard realised a series of rectangular greens connected by a conventional road network.

The late 1930s and early 1940s was perhaps the most experimental time for Velarde as an architect. The hiatus of the Second World War and his ill health encouraged a greater flexibility; he entered the burgeoning field of schools, and made digressions overseas and into housing. Thereafter he concentrated again on churches, for although with Reilly's death Velarde lost his mentor and greatest publicist – the journal articles dried up – the commissions for churches increased.

5 Post-war churches

Velarde's career was interrupted during the war and for many years thereafter. The economic cost of the conflict was enormous in the loss of export trade and in American dollars, which in turn restricted imports such as timber. With a fragile economy and a shortage of building materials, construction was controlled by licences until November 1954 and directed towards public housing, schools and industry. Few licences were granted to churches. Velarde wrote to Charles Reilly in 1946 that he 'was very busy but not building'.[1]

The war years were not an entirely empty time, however. Velarde's teaching at Liverpool University continued, and he worked on housing and entered competitions, as well as building and extending schools. In May 1947 he came second in an international competition for a new Anglican cathedral for Colombo in Sri Lanka. The assessor, Sir Giles Scott, commented that 'it has a certain grandeur relying on simple surfaces, both inside and out, that would create an impressive effect'. Curiously, however, he regarded its plan – with an exactly square nave surrounded by aisles and entrances on three sides, and with a long Lady Chapel behind the high altar – as 'more suitable for a Mosque than a Christian Cathedral'.[2]

Velarde's first post-war church was St Aidan of Lindisfarne, for the new parish of Huyton created in 1948. Such was the shortage of materials that he adapted a former RAF aircraft hangar, probably brought from the air base at Burtonwood, adding a porch, sanctuary and two sacristies. Archbishop Downey consecrated it in July 1949. A large, 'grand' church was never built because of the pressure to provide schools in the parish, also realised by Velarde. When in 1988 falling rolls made the infants' school redundant, the parish priest suggested that the building be adapted as a new church. Velarde's school hall became the nave of the new church, converted by Peter Moore of the Pozzoni Design Group in 1990–2. Velarde's little hanger church was then demolished. Pews from his St Aloysius, Roby, made surplus by the reordering there, were brought to the new St Aidan's.[3]

The building of housing estates in Huyton and Roby prompted the division of the area into seven parishes. That of St Aloysius was first

St Winefride's RC church, Monksmoor, Shrewsbury

proposed in 1934 when a temporary church opened. The parish was formally created in 1936 and the priest, Fr Michael J O'Sullivan, commissioned a permanent church. The foundation stone for St Aloysius, Roby, was laid on 10 September 1939, but building work was then shelved. Velarde worked on schools for Fr O'Sullivan throughout the last years of the war, and finally got his chance to build a new church when the Liverpool Joint Advisory Board selected O'Sullivan as the recipient for the one new Roman Catholic Church to be given permission, endorsed by Archbishop Downey 'as a mark of my personal appreciation of all you have done, and are doing, to solve the problem of school accommodation in the district'. A new foundation stone was laid on 10 September 1949, exactly ten years after the first, but work began in earnest only in 1950 and Bishop Halsall consecrated the completed church in April 1952.[4]

Although a relatively modest building, the final cost was £57,777. It was unusual in Velarde's work, for the exposed concrete arches supporting the roof are slightly pointed, although the arcades have his customary round arches. It is also unusual in being rendered internally, a reflection of the poor bricks available in the aftermath of the war. Fr O'Sullivan installed a vintage organ in 1954. The church was reordered in 1992 by the Vis Williams Partnership, when a nave altar was erected in front of the sanctuary railings, but most of the original fittings remain, including the stone high altar with a curving canopy set into the east sanctuary arch, the astylar marble sanctuary railings, a stone drum font and original wooden benches.[5]

Our Lady of Pity, Greasby, 1951–1952

The first important post-war church commission was in the Diocese of Shrewsbury. Situated on the Wirral halfway between the Dee and Mersey coasts, Greasby had been a quiet rural village until the opening of the Mersey (Queensway) Tunnel in 1934 and improvements to the ferry and rail services opened up the area to commuter housing. A site for a church was acquired on Mill Lane in 1940, and the parish priest from Upton began holding services in an army hut moved from Heswall, where it had been used as a church since 1919. Fr John Murphy, Velarde's friend since schooldays, was appointed as the first priest of the new Greasby parish in 1944.[6] He quickly commissioned a new church.[7] He became Bishop of Shrewsbury in 1949 but returned to lay the foundation stone in May 1951 and again for the opening in July 1952. The celebratory luncheon that day featured a 42-pound cake made by the nuns of Upton Convent in the shape of the new building.[8]

Although not a large church, the composition attempts a show of grandeur towards the street. The gable of the narthex at the liturgical west end (in reality facing east), is linked to a campanile by a single-storey arcade that serves pragmatically to restrict access to the presbytery courtyard and

Our Lady of Pity RC church, Greasby

visually to unify the composition. The nave and sanctuary occupy a rectangular box below a shallow pitched roof. The external buttresses along the nave were a late addition as building began, prompted by fears that the thrust of the internal arches might push out the side walls. The round-headed windows, originally with blue-green tinted glass but now clear (in uPVC frames), are curiously arranged, with one upper window set over a lower pair linked by fluted cast mullions.

Internally, the church is impressive, a single space comprising a five-bay nave and single-bay sanctuary defined by six powerful semicircular brick arches. The ceiling of flat plaster panels is currently painted white but was originally a Velardian blue. The sanctuary is only three steps above the nave, adding to the simple connection between the congregation and celebrant. The communion rails have been removed, but the altar, tabernacle and a fine polyptych of the Crucifixion with Our Lady and St John flanked by angels all display Velarde's distinctive style; the polyptych was taken down as part of the reordering, but was restored and reinstated in the 1990s.

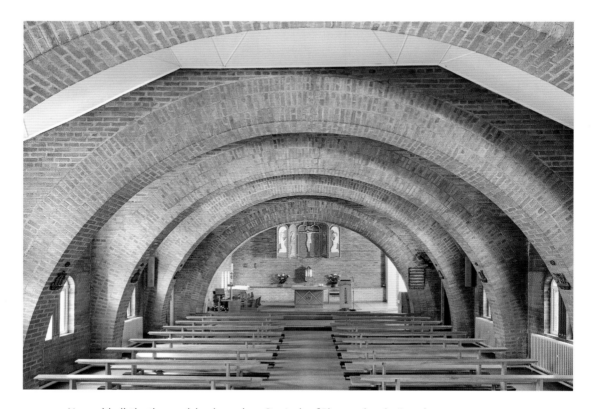

Nave with distinctive semicircular arches, Our Lady of Pity RC church, Greasby

Greasby offered a template for Velarde's medium-sized post-war churches – those not large enough for a galleried choir or double-height nave, but capable of delivering a sense of drama. He created intensity by a combination of a low, brick vault and richly decorated fittings in gold, orange and blue that provided accents of strong colour in the most important places. The expensive two-inch bricks of the 1930s gave way to standard sizes set in stretcher bond, but games of scale were still played with the unexpectedly small windows, the upper row giving a partly concealed source of light. A campanile with a pyramidal copper top became a feature of all Velarde's significant post-war churches outside London.

English Martyrs, Wallasey, 1951–1953

The grandest of all Velarde's post-war churches and the epitome of his mature style, English Martyrs ranks with St Monica's as Velarde's most important work. The size of the church permitted a number of ideas trialled at St Monica's, such as the choir gallery, asymmetric aisles and multiple windows. As at St Monica's there is a completeness to the composition, with the fittings and art works created under his supervision and most of them surviving.

Belonging to another Wirral parish in the Diocese of Shrewsbury, its origins date back to 1901, with a temporary corrugated iron church erected in 1907. Throughout the 1920s and 1930s the congregation raised money for a permanent church, and in 1937 commissioned the prolific local architects Edmund Kirby & Sons to produce a design. Tenders were received in 1939, but building was stopped with the outbreak of war. A new scheme was commissioned in 1950 from Velarde, perhaps on the recommendation of the newly appointed Bishop Murphy. The foundation stone was finally laid on 4 May 1952 and the completed church opened on 31 August 1953, at a cost of £50,000.

English Martyrs looks more striking for being set in an established early 20th-century residential district rather than among housing of its own age. It features the expanses of fine brickwork typical of Velarde's work, with bold, simple masses expressing each element of the church and rising to a semi-detached campanile. The building is orientated north–south on a sloping site, with the liturgical east end to the north and a steep drop of some ten feet towards playing fields to the west, where a presbytery was built in 1956. The church is faced in grey-brown brick, set in Velarde's favourite English garden wall bond in the nave, low aisles and campanile, and stretcher bond for the projecting baptistery and porch. The pitched roofs of the nave and sanctuary are continuous, without even the small step seen at St Monica's. There are no parapets to the main body, and the absence of rainwater goods helps to reinforce the abstraction of the plain brick façades. As at St

English Martyrs' RC church, Wallasey, viewed from the south-east

Gabriel's, Velarde went to considerable lengths of detailed design here to avoid their presence on principal elevations.[9]

The composition to St George's Road creates a sense of place, for the tall campanile and low baptistery bookend a small piazza, with arcading imitating a feature found in medieval buildings where a further aisle could have been lost, or perhaps could yet be added. The entrance is adjacent to the baptistery, with a second porch on the opposite side of the nave no longer used. The most distinctive element is the campanile, which changes at high level from a square plan in brick to an octagonal open belfry in stone, topped by a copper cupola. The nave fenestration is curious: round-headed windows are punched into the brickwork in two banks of four, forming a cruciform pattern, separated by two single windows.[10] The single-storey aisle has a blind arcade with cast statues of the English Martyrs set centrally in each bay, but no windows. These and a larger pietà on the south face of the campanile are all by Philip Lindsey Clark.[11] Cast and carved sculptures are particularly prominent on the exterior here, and feature as mullions in the window arrays to the sanctuary and paired windows to the

94

Main entrance to the west front of English Martyrs RC church, photographed upon completion in 1953

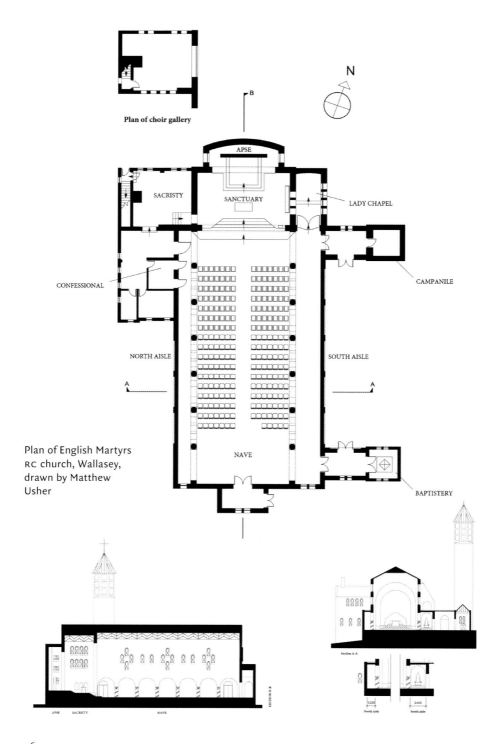

Plan of choir gallery

N

APSE

SACRISTY

SANCTUARY

LADY CHAPEL

CONFESSIONAL

CAMPANILE

NORTH AISLE

SOUTH AISLE

A — A

Plan of English Martyrs
RC church, Wallasey,
drawn by Matthew
Usher

NAVE

BAPTISTERY

APSE   SACRISTY   NAVE

SECTION B-B

Section A-A

1220   2440

North aisle   South aisle

Detail of nave window pattern and pietà at the base of the campanile, English Martyrs RC church

baptistery and its link corridor. To the west end, a large rose window incorporates a cast stone cross overlaid with a relief of Christ, again by Clark.

As in most of the later Velarde churches the interior is also faced in exposed brickwork. The upper walls of the nave are supported on seven-bay arcades, their round-arch openings continuing the modern Romanesque theme of the fenestration, which is repeated in the great double arches to the sanctuary and high altar. The arcades are supported on round concrete columns incised with silver-painted spirals under vestigial cushion capitals marked by crosses; never again would Velarde adopt the internal buttress cut by passage aisles found in his pre-war churches. One feature repeated from St Monica's, however, is the choir gallery set to the side of the sanctuary, here with a single round-arched opening inset with a bronze balustrade still broadly Art Deco in spirit. The angled roofs of the nave and chancel, supported on exposed steel beams, are both decorated with chevrons of silver and orange, the latter repeated on the flat ceilings of the aisles. The sanctuary is raised up six steps, originally behind a low communion rail (now gone), with the altar up a further three steps and backed by a triangular

Nave of English Martyrs RC church, Wallasey

Altar with carved angel by Herbert Tyson Smith, English Martyrs RC church

stone reredos carved with reliefs of the 12 disciples looking up to Christ at the apex. The reredos is slightly forward of the east wall, where there hangs a large metal crucifixion. The altar itself has been moved further forward and reduced in length, but it retains Velarde's tapered base decorated with a silver angel proffering a chalice.

The (liturgical) north aisle terminates in a Lady Chapel illuminated by four round-headed windows, with an altar by Herbert Tyson Smith. The baptistery placed symbolically by the entrance is no longer in use but remains complete. There are more Tyson Smith carvings round the square font, set on another tapered base, this time of angels chasing the Devil; the pyramidal cover is carved with fish scales and capped with a gilt cross.

Baptistery and font, English Martyrs RC church

Here the ceiling is decorated in orange with silver and blue ribs, while the adjoining lobby has a pattern of blue and white diamonds on an orange background. The range of geometric painted patterns to the ceilings at English Martyrs shows Velarde at his most playful. Indeed, the austere brick interiors are enriched by a wealth of decorative detail, in ceilings, metalwork and carved angels – Velarde was clearly making the most of his post-war opportunities, and a bigger budget.

St Cuthbert by the Forest, Mouldsworth, 1953–1955

Velarde's smallest church, and his only truly rural scheme, was designed to seat a congregation of just 72 people. The land around the straggling village of Mouldsworth, on the edge of the Cheshire plain, was largely arable. In 1926 an influx of seasonal workers from Ireland prompted the landlady of the Station Hotel, Margaret Spann, to persuade a curate out from St Werburgh's, Chester, to say Mass in a wooden pavilion in her garden. As more Irish farm workers settled permanently in the area, so the monthly Mass became weekly and, after the Second World War, Mrs Spann bought the site from the Northgate Brewery and presented it to the Diocese of Shrewsbury. Canon Hugh Welch from St Werburgh's (also a supporter of his school building) commissioned Velarde to prepare plans in 1953 following local fundraising. The church, dedicated by Bishop Murphy in 1955, cost just £7,000, reflecting the tiny scale of this building compared to English Martyrs', Wallasey. The detached campanile was added to the design in 1954 at a cost of another £1,000, but a pietà intended for it was never realised. 'By the Forest' was added to the dedication in 2000, and references Delemere Forest, one of three great medieval forests in Cheshire.[12]

The church sits towards the bottom of a sloping site. Approaching the village from the south, the campanile with its distinctive copper and stone cupola and the tiled church roof are the dominant features. The campanile resembles those at St Teresa's, Upholland, and later small churches around Shrewsbury, except that here the walls are slightly battered, a subtle difference giving an illusion of height lacking in the later examples. Arriving at the church the other distinctive feature is the narthex with its paired gables and diamond windows. By drawing upon ideas trialled at Our Lady of Pity, Greasby, Velarde created a strong sense of place out of a small structure.

Traditional in plan, the four-bay nave is again articulated with sloping buttresses externally and terminates in a blind, semicircular apse. The sanctuary is illuminated by side windows in a variant of Velarde's usual form, being composed of diamonds like those in the narthex. Internally the bays of the aisle-less grey brick nave are divided by pointed arches in a scaled-down and Gothicised version of Greasby. The windows to each bay are paired, with cast angel mullions, but with pointed rather than round arches. This

St Cuthbert by the Forest RC church, Mouldsworth, viewed from the south-east

novel feature, with only St Aloysius offering something of a precedent, gives St Cuthbert's an Arts and Crafts feel in the fashion of W R Lethaby. The altar is a simple gilt relief design, not unlike that at the near-contemporary St Teresa's, Upholland. Most of the other original fittings were salvaged or gifted because of the very tight budget. Mrs Spann donated a rather large organ, now removed, while the chairs were sourced from older churches but replaced by pews in the 1990s since they brought with them an infestation of woodworm; the Stations of the Cross came from the South Tyrol.[13]

Velarde repeated the Greasby formula at two further churches, both in the Shrewsbury suburbs: St Winefride's, Monkmoor, in 1956, and Our Lady of Pity, Harlescott, in 1957–61. Both are notable for their handsome little campaniles and apsed sanctuaries. Our Lady of Pity, completed after Velarde's death, shows changes made by O'Mahony and the successor practice, for instead of coloured ceiling panels there is varnished boarding – a rather awkward compromise between two men's ideas. Velarde also designed much plainer churches for the Diocese of Shrewsbury, including St Gabriel's, Alsager, from 1953, and the demolished St Mary Magdalene, Much

Nave of St Cuthbert by the Forest RC church, Mouldsworth

St Winefride's RC church, Monksmoor, Shrewsbury, altar and sanctuary

Wenlock, of 1955, described by John Tarn, a former Head of Architecture at Liverpool University, as 'the next step on from the mission hut'.[14]

St Teresa's, Upholland, 1955–1957

St Teresa's lies at the heart of a rural area with a long tradition of Catholic recusancy, on the northern edge of the Lancashire village of Upholland near Wigan, adjacent to St Joseph's Seminary which closed in 1996. The parish of Upholland, planned since 1940, separated from that of St James, Orrell, in 1955, although Velarde began producing drawings for a church as early as 1952.[15] Constructed between 1955 and 1957, this is one of his richest designs, displaying confident brick massing, stylised round-headed windows and high-quality internal decoration.

The building is dramatic from a distance since, by pushing the church towards the rear of the site, Velarde enables its form to be seen up a rising slope framed against the sky. As at St Cuthbert by the Forest, the careful placement generates the maximum visual impact from a relatively small mass. The adjacent parish hall and presbytery by Velarde are contemporary, although of little architectural interest.

The semi-detached campanile has a belfry topped by three rows of round-arched openings set in ashlar stone under a copper-clad pyramidal roof crowned by a gilded cross – a marriage of tradition and the influence of Dominikus Böhm. A series of small diamond windows climb up the tower following the access stair, showing Velarde revelling once again in seemingly erratic, asymmetrical elements. The link connecting the campanile continues along the body of the church as a single low aisle – blind, but marking the five-bay division of the nave with buttresses topped by cast stone figures of English saints – and terminates as the entrance and Galilee porch wrapped around the ritual west end. The nave projects above with a plain tile pitched roof tucked behind a very low parapet, again with no visible gutters. Pairs of round-headed windows provide a clerestory to the nave with a double array lighting the sanctuary from the south; there are larger windows on the opposite side where there is no aisle, exaggerating the asymmetry.

Our Lady of Pity RC church, Harlescott, Shrewsbury

St Teresa's RC church, Upholland, view from the south-east

Drawing by Giles Velarde of the east elevation of St Teresa's RC church, Upholland

The interior is too low to permit a gallery even for a small choir, who instead occupy the shallow sanctuary. The single aisle is defined by a brick arcade of round arches supported on circular columns clad in gold mosaic and with cast capitals painted blue. Gold and blue dominate the colour scheme, for the altar's broad legs are carved with gold angels, while the reredos is a gold and blue triptych of Christ flanked by angels set in an orange framework. The ceiling repeats the blue of the aisle capitals, with silver chevrons. Pairs of windows in the nave are separated by angel mullions and some have blue glass, so that all of Velarde's favourite colours and motifs are here in abundance. A small chapel at the end of the aisle and a baptistery – replete with a square font – complete the principal internal spaces, all of which are in exceptionally good and near original condition. In his article for the *Clergy Review*, Velarde suggested that the baptistery go in the bottom of the tower, and this became a feature of his smaller, late churches.[16]

Nave with single side aisle, St Teresa's RC church, Upholland

Altar, triptych and sanctuary, St Teresa's RC church, Upholland

It was this church that first brought Velarde's post-war work to the attention of Historic England (then English Heritage) and the Twentieth Century Society, and it became his first post-1945 church to be listed, in December 1999.

St Alexander's, Brasenose Road, Bootle, 1954–1957

A new parish was created to serve the docklands community of Kirkdale, on the boundary of Bootle and Liverpool, in 1862. Bishop Goss of Liverpool laid the foundation stone of St Alexander's church, the dedication being to his own patron saint, and opened an enormous and ornate church by E W Pugin in 1867, which was extended in 1884. It was almost entirely destroyed in the air raids of May 1941. Archbishop Godfrey laid the foundation stone of Velarde's replacement on the same site in June 1955, a church designed for 500 people at a cost of £90,000, mostly paid by the War Damage Commission.[17] Archbishop Heenan opened the completed church in July 1957.

This very large church had the most dramatic of Velarde's later exteriors, thanks to its twin towers, Romanesque in character, but with distinctive

West front of St Alexander's RC church, Bootle (demolished 1991)

elements that he was to repeat at Holy Cross, Bidston. These include the use of Portland stone as a contrast to red brick for the upper parts of the towers, featuring Velarde's distinctive round-arched openings under conical copper tops and gilded crosses. A baptistery, top-lit under its own sharp-pointed cone, is set on the north side of the long *Westwerk*, near-blind save for the bold teak doors. Bands of fenestration illuminated the spacious interior, 162 feet (49.4m) long, 58 feet (17.7m) wide and 35 feet (10.7m) high. Again, round-arched arcades shielded uneven aisles, supported on round, tapered columns finished in gold leaf. The wooden ceilings were also ablaze with gold and bright colours, while the terrazzo floors were inlaid with gold mosaic and coloured emblems. Here, however, there was one novel feature: the placement of the Lady Chapel directly behind the main altar – claimed to be 'Old English' in derivation and separated by a light and elegant bronze screen that supported a carved wooden Calvary. The main altar was in white stone and the mensa was supported by two carved pillars each depicting an angelic figure, with a communion rail in light gold bronze.[18] The church, together with the adjoining Victorian school that had survived the bombing, was demolished in 1991, and all that survives is Pugin's presbytery, converted to offices and lost in a sea of run-down warehousing so extensive that it is hard to imagine there was ever a vast, close-knit community living here.

The Shrine of Our Lady of Lourdes, Blackpool, 1955–1957

Our Lady of Lourdes is not a parish church, but a chapel dedicated to the Virgin Mary, established in thanks for the relatively light damage sustained by the Diocese of Lancaster in the Second World War. Bishop Thomas Flynn wrote in September 1945 how, 'as the danger became more acute, and one diocese after another suffered terrible losses in life and property, I asked for earnest prayers to our patroness, Our Lady of Lourdes … and we were marvellously spared'.[19] The shrine was constructed between 1955 and 1957 by a local builder, William Eaves, who also donated the land. Contributions came from every parish in the diocese. The location was chosen because Blackpool was at the centre of the diocese, and there were good bus services from the town centre to the adjoining hospital.

As built, the Shrine was entirely faced in Portland stone. It was the only instance of Velarde entirely departing from his beloved brick, and its whiteness enhances the impression of a jewelled casket. A small copper spire is placed centrally on the apex of the four-bay nave, which has a steeply pitched copper roof. The end gable features an impressive large low-relief sculpture of the Trinity, carved *in situ* by David John and three assistants; they were also responsible for four statues that form pinnacles at the building's four corners, taking one each. Robin Riley, one of the assistants, recalled working with Velarde. When asked 'how he wanted a detail carved,

Sign erected on the site for the Thanksgiving
Shrine of Our Lady of Lourdes, Blackpool, 1955

Thanksgiving Shrine of Our Lady of Lourdes,
Blackpool

Velarde replied "make it something like this", meaning, of course, "make
it exactly like this".[20] The aisles, almost as tall as the nave, have bands of
windows comprising alternating squares of quatrefoil and cross-patterned
tracery, a variant of Velarde's earlier work but filled with characteristic pale-
tinted glass. He had noticed that if a sheet of Pilkington's blue-tinted glass
was set beside a sheet of white, the white looked just a little pink, and this
contrast became a feature of his last churches.

Internally the round columns clad in gold mosaic are almost identical
to those at St Teresa's, but here they support round arches with a
rendered finish, a motif repeated in the chancel arch, sanctuary arch
and all the smaller door openings, bringing a remarkable geometric
consistency to the space. A characteristic nave ceiling of blue panels set
in gold frames is repeated in the sanctuary with red panels. David John
carved the reredos and altar, presumably to Velarde's designs given his

ELEVATION TO ROAD

IN HONOUR OF OUR LADY.
CHAPEL AT BLACKPOOL
FOR MY LORD BISHOP OF LANCASTER

F. X. VELARDE B. ARCH. F. R. I. B. A.

Velarde's drawing of the west front of the Thanksgiving Shrine of Our Lady of Lourdes, Blackpool

David John and assistants carving, *in situ*, the sculpture of the Holy Trinity to the west front of the Thanksgiving Shrine of Our Lady of Lourdes, Blackpool

One of four corner statues carved for the Thanksgiving Shrine of Our Lady of Lourdes, Blackpool

Nave of the Thanksgiving Shrine of Our Lady of Lourdes, Blackpool

youth.[21] The bronze altar rails are Art Deco abstractions of a chalice and wafer, symbols of the communion. The floor is tiled throughout with inset cross motifs.

The wealth of materials and the extensive carvings account for the high cost of this small building, at £59,000 proportionately his most expensive post-war work. Robin Riley asked why so much time and effort was spent on the timber boarding that was due to be covered by the copper roofing, to be told by Velarde, 'Just think of the memory of it'.[22] Here is a total work of art and architecture. It was managed by nuns from the Congregation of Adoration of Marie Reparatrice, who opened a convent next door in 1956, until in 1994 it passed to the Blessed Sacrament Fathers. The shrine's mission was relocated to St Winifred's, Preston, and the building closed in 1999, when it was threatened with total demolition. Listing was achieved in just 48 hours, a record for any post-war building. It was transferred to the Historic Chapels Trust in 2002, who have carried out some repairs to the exterior.

Holy Cross, Bidston, 1957–1959

The last church entirely completed by Velarde before his death in December 1960 was also his personal favourite.[23] Fundraising by the parish began in 1954, to replace a temporary building that had been serving the growing suburb of North Birkenhead since 1929, on land originally set aside for a public library. Velarde had already designed the Catholic primary school associated with the church in 1947 and was the obvious choice of architect. Design work started in 1955 and the foundation stone was laid by Bishop Murphy on 12 October 1957. Holy Cross was consecrated on 11 June 1959, having cost £87,000 including fittings.[24]

The design shows Velarde's work continuing to evolve, in which the basic components remained the same but new arrangements emerged inside and out. The (liturgical) west end and the top of the campanile are clad in Portland stone, but otherwise this is a brick building with a long nave under a tiled roof, with low side aisles and a projecting Lady Chapel. The land rises slightly, so the east end is sunk into the side of the hill, while the ceremonial entrance is lifted by five steps. It is this west end that differs most from Velarde's earlier churches, consisting of a central stone cube flanked to the left by a secondary, smaller cube containing the day-to-day entrance, and to the right by the tower containing the baptistery within its base. Slender stone pinnacles with finials and crosses top the corners of the central cube, an effect somewhat resembling the Brno Crematorium of 1930 by Ernst Wiesner, a colleague at the university from 1950. This elevation disturbed Pevsner, who described it as an 'overscaled toy fort tower' though the revised edition is kinder.[25]

Holy Cross RC church, Bidston, altar and sanctuary photographed in 1959

As is often the case, it is the interior that delights. The first surprise is immediate, with an entrance lobby clad entirely in striking red and black diamond patterns of mosaic. The relative darkness of this space is lifted by a tall, conical skylight. The porch leads into the narthex, which is also clad entirely in mosaics, this time in a bold black and white chequerboard pattern inlaid with cross motifs in gold. The effect is almost post-modern. To one side, at the base of the tower, is the baptistery in red and white diamond mosaics inlaid with fish and hands in Velarde's favourite gold. Light, abstracted metal screen doors allow the baptistery to be visible from the lobby through the narthex, and this run of fully mosaic-clad spaces provides a highly original and dramatic entrance sequence unlike anything previously seen in his work.

All these exuberant patterns are, however, only a foretaste for the drama of the body of the church. The nave and sanctuary are combined, without a chancel arch, under a panelled blue and gold ceiling, terminating in an apse.

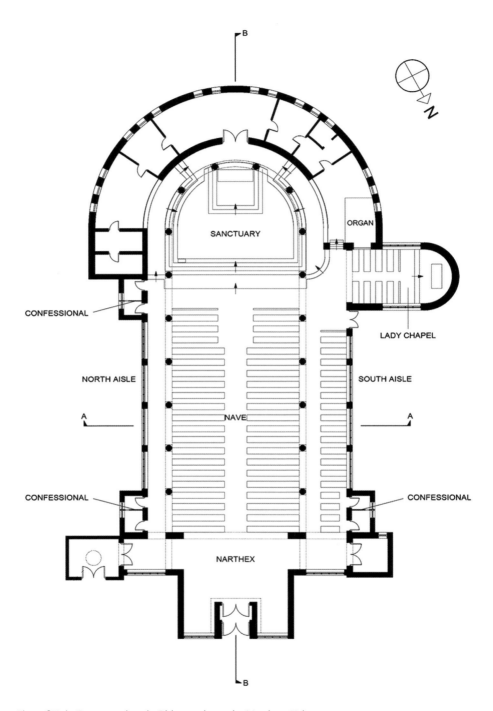

Plan of Holy Cross RC church, Bidston, drawn by Matthew Usher

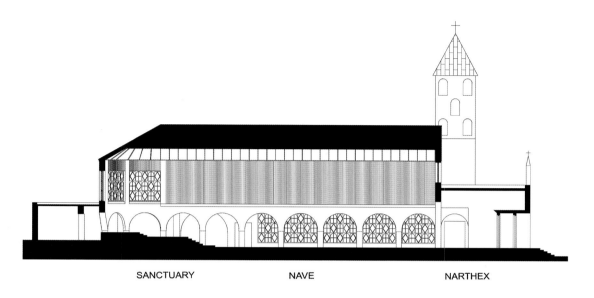

SANCTUARY   NAVE   NARTHEX

Holy Cross RC church, Bidston, section through nave and sanctuary, drawn by Matthew Usher

The lower half of the space is clad in travertine, the upper parts in fluted plaster – why Velarde abandoned his usual preference for a brick interior is unknown, but he concealed fluorescent tubes behind the cornice of the travertine that would have accentuated the fluting. The aisles are connected by an ambulatory that ran round the apse, all defined by a continuous arcade of semicircular arches supported on round columns. These columns have no capitals, not even the minimal, stylised versions found at Blackpool, though they are again clad in mosaic. The Stations of the Cross, carved in relief and heightened with gold, came from another church. The side aisles, again asymmetrical, are illuminated by a continuous band of geometric window arrays, alternating rectangular and round-headed lights filled with Velarde's characteristic tinted glass. Above the ambulatory at high level five similar window arrays flood the sanctuary platform with light. Two flights of six and three steps lead up to the altar, although the low, light, chrome-plated communion rail was removed in the one act of reordering undertaken here. The semicircular apse and ambulatory are reminiscent of early Romanesque basilicas and the single volume of the main worship space suggested that – like other architects in the vanguard of the Liturgical Movement – Velarde was returning to the earliest Christian worship for inspiration.

    Outside the ambulatory are spaces for the choir and organ, and a children's room. The Lady Chapel is set at right angles to the body of the

Mosaics to the narthex and baptistery, Holy Cross RC church, Bidston

Nave viewed towards the sanctuary in 2002, with the semicircular ambulatory behind the altar, Holy Cross RC church, Bidston

church. This simple space, with its own apse, is encrusted with the most spectacular mosaics: every surface is clad in blue tesserae, set in a diamond pattern with gold highlights. The focal point is a representation of Our Lady and the Christ Child, seated and flanked by angels. Designed by Velarde and made by Art Pavements, a subsidiary of Carter's of Poole, this echoed the early churches of Byzantium and Ravenna. The ceiling repeats the pattern of the nave but with a gold star over the altar.

This highly idiosyncratic and original church closed in July 2006 and has remained boarded up ever since.[26] That such a fine building should be at risk is a cause of great concern. The font has been relocated to Woodchurch and altar frontals are now in the Williamson Art Gallery and Museum, but otherwise the church survives for the moment, though prey to vandalism.

Detail of mosaics, Lady Chapel, Holy Cross RC church, Bidston

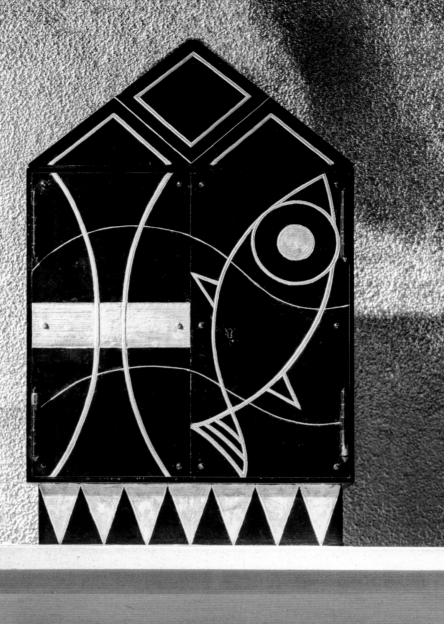

6 The London churches

A Liverpool-based practice, busy with schools as well as churches in the north-west of England and never with a staff exceeding 12, seems an unlikely choice for the Diocese of Westminster.[1] Yet from the mid-1950s to his death, Velarde undertook a series of important buildings there. One contact was Archbishop Godfrey, who had served as Archbishop of Liverpool in 1953–6, but he had notably unadventurous tastes in art and architecture.[2] More important was Father Gurrin SJ of Farm Street, a friend and, according to Janet Gnosspelius, one of Velarde's former schoolmasters.

Velarde designed a chapel and four churches in the diocese, three of which were completed by his assistants after his death. This work now appears as a swan-song to his career, yet despite Velarde's generally poor health there was no reason at the time to suspect that this would not be a new phase for an architect with potentially 15 or even 20 more years left to practice.

The first southern commission was a small chapel for the Grail Society. This was a lay community of Dutch origins, formed of Roman Catholic women who followed a collective life of dedication without taking Holy Orders. Following the Eucharistic Congress of 1932, Cardinal Vaughan invited the Grail to open a London chapter, which was led by two founder members, Baroness Yvonne Bosch van Drakestein and Lydwine van Kersbergen. Baroness van Drakestein stayed in Britain when the English chapter was declared autonomous in 1949, having in 1947 acquired Waxwell Farmhouse, a building on the edge of London at Pinner. Late 16th-century in origin, the farmhouse is set in eight acres (3.2ha) of gardens, and in 1957 a new accommodation wing and chapel were added. Velarde was the architect for the chapel, introduced to Baroness van Drakestein through Fr Gurrin sometime in late 1954.

The chapel, seating 60, links the new wing to the 16th-century building and its bricks match those of the original farmhouse, with a plain tile roof. The land slopes away towards the garden and a series of service rooms are tucked underneath the sanctuary. Gnosspelius recalled settling many of the detailed drawings with Velarde in the lounge of the Exchange Hotel in

Tabernacle, St Luke's RC church, Pinner

Liverpool, convenient for trains to Formby.[3] Internally the single rectangular space has a semicircular apse with a line of Velarde's distinctive windows set high on one side. The walls are lined in rough plaster and the principal decoration is the brightly coloured gold, orange and blue diamond-patterned ceiling. The marble altar sits on a terrazzo plinth two steps up from the congregation, and contains a relic of St Thomas Becket, who stayed at the Archbishop of Canterbury's manor house at Harrow two weeks before his martyrdom.[4] A tapestry of the Last Supper by the Dutch artist Luc van Hoeck hangs in the apse, whilst a stained glass window designed by Giles Velarde remains un-executed.[5] At the opposite end are Stations of the Cross by Caryll Houselander.[6] It is the small touches that are most important: the water stoops, candleholders and the tabernacle with its fish motif catch the eye.

The Chapel of the Grail Society, Pinner

Altar and sanctuary window, The Grail Society, Pinner

Drawing by Giles Velarde of an un-executed stained glass window, The Grail Society, Pinner

Tapestry of The Last Supper by Luc van Hoeck, The Grail Society, Pinner

The Grail moved to Winchester in 2012, and in 2014 Waxwell was taken over by SPEC (Spiritual and Personal Encounter with Christ) as a youth retreat centre for the Diocese of Westminster.

St Luke's, Pinner, 1957–1958

This is the largest and grandest of Velarde's London churches. He found a kindred spirit at St Luke's in Fr Wilfrid Trotman, who had studied at the Royal College of Music before entering the priesthood. They were introduced through Baroness van Drakestein in the spring of 1955.

A Catholic parish at Pinner was established in 1913, for which Percy Lamb (one of Bentley's assistants on Westminster Cathedral) designed a small church based on an earlier building at Chalfont St Peter. The full scheme was illustrated in *The Builder* but only part was built.[7] It was extended in 1923 and a chapel dedicated to St Philomena added in 1931, but by the 1950s it had become too small and there were structural problems. Fr Trotman was a curate at Borehamwood, but was quickly transferred when the priest at Pinner, Fr Frederick Lyngnane, died suddenly in 1954. The diocese demanded that he oversee the building of a new church.[8] Fr Trotman blessed the completed church on 16 November 1957, but the formal opening was on 19 January 1958 by Archbishop Godfrey.

Costing £46,000, a modest sum by the late 1950s, St Luke's is bold but simpler than Velarde's most ambitious Merseyside churches. A typical basilica in plan, seating 350 worshippers, the exterior is dominated by a strong *Westwerk* topped by twin copper-clad towers with open belfries. This liturgical west end (actually facing east) has the most Germanic feel of all Velarde's buildings. It is more severe than St Monica's, Bootle, relieved only by two statues in Portland stone of the Virgin Mary and St Luke, carved by David John; the mastiff at Mary's feet is Fr Trotman's dog Punch.[9] The side aisles have Velarde's characteristic multi-panel arrays of rectangular and round-headed windows with small square apertures at high level into the nave. St Luke's was unusual among Velarde's works in its great lightness, part of Fr Trotman's brief. Gnosspelius recalled discussing the clerestory windows with Velarde, suggesting round-headed windows as harmonious with the rest. 'I don't want it to be too perfect, Janet', was his reply, and the final windows were almost square in shape. With hindsight she accepted that 'a little discord would add, as it might be, a little piquancy to the sauce'.[10]

While externally the language of brick and copper, towers and *Westwerk*, window arrays and tinted glass are typical of Velarde, internally changes in approach can be detected. The porch opens into a full-height narthex, with a Lady Chapel on the north side and a baptistery to the south. The former has a circular skylight, and all are in white-painted

West front, St Luke's, Pinner

Nave of St Luke's, Pinner

Lady Chapel, St Luke's, Pinner

Opposite: Water stoop with fish insert in brass, St Luke's, Pinner

brick with deep blue ceilings. The nave is exceptionally simple and light, designed for music and to enable Trotman's choirs to read their scores. It is lined in painted brick, with round-arched arcades springing from circular columns clad in gold mosaic under a ceiling of celotex ceiling boards painted in two shades of blue and inset with troughs of fluorescent lighting (an opening brochure describes a 'lilac tint'). The effect is to turn a simple rectangular box into a complex play of form and colour, for the nave ceiling pattern continues uninterrupted into the sanctuary and down the east end wall behind the altar. Ceiling and wall merge. There are five steps between the nave and sanctuary, but without a chancel arch there is little other differentiation now that a light communion rail has been removed. As at Velarde's other large churches, the organ and choir are elevated to a gallery, compressing the spatial relationship between the priest and his congregation.

Here we see Velarde moving from an architecture defined by mass and form to a lighter touch, suggesting the influence of Scandinavian modernism. Colour comes to the fore. The attention to detail and integration of works of art, including the tabernacle and sculptures by David John, remain a constant. Every opportunity for symbolic detail is taken, down to incised brass fishes inlaid within the stone holy water stoops. The pews

were inspired by Hector Corfiato's at Notre Dame de France, Leicester Place, completed in 1955 and which Velarde found comfortable and economical; he sent Gnosspelius to measure them in February 1957.[11] The builder for all Velarde's London churches was William Lacey of Hounslow.

St Teresa of the Child Jesus, Borehamwood, Hertfordshire, 1959–1962
Fr Trotman introduced Velarde to Fr J A Murray at St Teresa's, where he had served as a curate in 1952–4. The first drawings date from 1959.[12] Smaller than St Luke's, Pinner, this design also employs a *Westwerk* and towers with a blank gable intended to be enlivened by another large sculpture by David John. Drawings indicate a large representation of the Annunciation, which was never installed, and the simple crucifix there today is rather too small.[13] The towers lack a belfry, being simple and rectangular in plan, of stone capped with steeply pitched copper roofs. The west end is entirely without windows, for the narthex is illuminated by openings below the towers on the side elevations. The original solid timber doors, with a raised diamond pattern that relieved this austere facade, were replaced by lighter glass versions in the 1990s. Early designs placed the Lady Chapel at the west end, balancing the baptistery on the opposite side of the narthex as at St Luke's, but by February 1960 it had been moved to the east end and annotations

to the drawings indicate a turn through ninety degrees to place it at right angles to the sanctuary as at Holy Cross, Bidston.[14]

As at St Luke's, Pinner, the nave is illuminated by multi-paned window arrays in the aisles, leaving the higher walls of the nave blank. The continuous run of these low-level windows introduces a horizontal emphasis into the elevations in marked contrast to the verticality of Velarde's larger churches in Merseyside. The only other feature of note externally is the tall, copper-clad skylight over the altar of the Lady Chapel, whose conical form plays against the curved apse of the chapel in contrast to the rectilinear forms of the nave. A minor point, indicating the transitional nature of this church and its completion after Velarde's death, is the prominence of the rainwater goods on the elevations; clearly the master did not have sight of this detail.

The interior feels like a stripped-down version of St Luke's, a single space with low side aisles framed by circular columns clad in gold mosaic supporting shallow arches, with a flat ceiling that runs continuously through

St Teresa of the Child Jesus RC church, Borehamwood

Nave and sanctuary, St Teresa of the Child Jesus RC church, Borehamwood

the church. The sanctuary is raised up five steps and illuminated by the typical large multi-paned window array. The size of the church was sufficient to permit the choir to be moved into a gallery with a grilled opening into the body of space, set above the Lady Chapel. The walls are finished in painted brick, again imparting a light, Scandinavian feel.

Giles Velarde recounted that, after their father's death, his brother Julian asked Janet Gnosspelius to complete St Teresa's. However, she sought Giles's help with the Lady Chapel as she was not a Catholic, and he in turn brought in Stephen Sykes, his old tutor from the Chelsea School of Art to produce a low relief of Our Lady in glass-reinforced plastic (GRP) to go behind the altar. The chapel had also to be used on special occasions as an overspill to the main space, so Giles designed the seating to be reversible as in the Liverpool trams of his youth.[15] The overall composition of St Teresa's is typical of his father's late works, but without the fine detail and carefully crafted altarware the church is an incomplete example of his work.

Velarde began two further churches before his death. SS Vincent De Paul and Louise Demarillac RC church, was built in 1959–62 for the Spanish Fathers and demolished in 2005. It was followed by St Edmund of Canterbury, Whitton, a substantial church built for the Order of St Edmund in 1961–3 largely by Richard O'Mahony, with works of art by Norman Dilworth and a west window of Florentine red glass.[16] Shortly after Velarde's death, his son

Photograph of the model of SS Vincent De Paul and Louise Demarillac RC church, Potters Bar (demolished 2005)

St Edmund of Canterbury, Whitton, Twickenham

Julian wrote to William Holford reassuring him that all the outstanding commissions would be 'finished in the FXV way'.[17] To the extent that no changes were made to the layout or form of the buildings this was true, and his principal staff – Janet Gnosspelius and Richard O'Mahony – understood the nature of a Velarde church even though they could not impart the extra touches that make the earlier interiors so special.

7 Velarde's legacy

If I had gone about this article in another manner ... I might have taken it as a fault in Velarde's church buildings that they suffer from this limitation, that they are pieces of individual excellence rather than examples of a new school of thought, and I cannot honestly think of them inspiring imitations (using the word in its best sense) to successful emulation.[1]

F X Velarde has so far avoided fame. His reputation remains largely confined to the circles of those concerned with 20th-century church architecture. However, within this field he is highly regarded, his churches sought out by enthusiasts. We hope the list of works provides some new ones to explore. Yet the thread was nearly lost, with his archive largely destroyed and those who knew him personally nearly all gone. Establishing the extent of his output has been the work of a detective. And of Velarde the man? But for the assistance of his younger son Giles, that aspect of this study would have been almost impossible.

Why has it taken so long, nearly 60 years since his death, for FXV to be recognised outside his specialism?

He had the friendship and promotion of the most powerful of allies in Charles Reilly, who until his death in 1948 ensured that Velarde's work was seen in exhibitions and journals at every opportunity. He had a secure and loyal client in the Catholic Church who kept him supplied with commissions for schools and churches. He had the support of dedicated staff like Janet Gnosspelius who many years later would accost architecture students in the corridors of Abercromby Square and berate them for their ignorance of his work.[2] He had a loving and close family who as his health failed became his chauffeurs and his legs.[3]

The clue lies in Reilly's prescient comment in 1938, that Velarde did not produce works that were part of a school of thought.

Some of the things that gave Velarde 'the rare quality of a sensitive originality', in the words of his friend Herbert Thearle, are his early adoption

Detail of nave column, English Martyrs' RC church, Wallasey

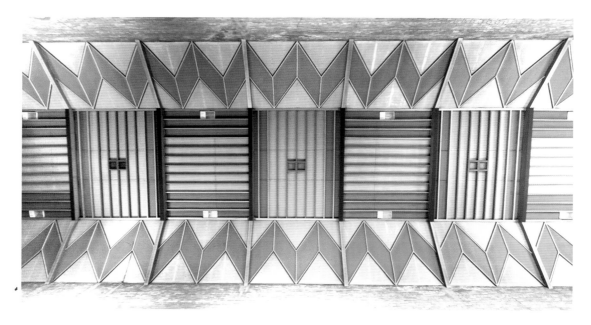

Ceiling to the nave of English Martyrs RC church

Carved angel to altar of St Gabriel's RC church, Alsager, Cheshire

of developments in European church architecture and liturgy and his deep integration of the work of artists and craftsmen in the realisation of his buildings.[4] With these attributes he establishes himself as an important outlier of Gavin Stamp's 'alternative modernism', even if it is one inspired by medievalism and Arts and Crafts traditions.[5] Velarde himself was not concerned with such categorisations; his comfort in his own work meant that he did not, unlike his contemporary Maxwell Fry or the later Liverpool graduate James Stirling, constantly reinvent himself. Velarde was a pragmatist when it came to stylistic loyalties, a man who had friends rather than associations.[6] His churches were similarly pieces of individual excellence, and after the war they became even more personal as the expressionist origins faded. The result by 1960 was that his architecture was almost out of time.

St Michael and All Angels RC church, Woodchurch, Wirral

Velarde was no polemicist. The little he wrote was specific to churches, focusing on continuity rather than revolution, and not challenging. This stress upon continuity would eventually leave him behind as reforming forces overtook the Catholic faith, leading to a new direction in the architecture of its churches endorsed by the Second Vatican Council. Velarde's assistant and eventual successor, Richard O'Mahony, the principal partner in the legacy practice, followed these new directions after Velarde's death. The churches started, but not completed, followed the established character of their forebears, but at St Michael and All Angels, Woodchurch, O'Mahony revised the plan as well as the materials radically to bring them into this new fashion. While the architectural press concentrated on the work of the New Churches Research Group, of which O'Mahony was a member, Velarde stands as a reminder of a lively alternative of colour and art that gave the Roman Catholic Church vitality through the 1950s and into the 1960s. This is what makes Velarde's work important. We can describe his colourful ceilings, his mosaics and love of gold, the sculpted altars, fonts and angel mullions, tall campaniles with their copper pyramid tops, and the mass of brickwork and round arches, yet fail to define a Velarde church. They are personal to him, an extension of his faith.

The trinity of Velarde's life and work were his churches, his Catholic faith and his family.

Notes

Introduction

1 Herbert Thearle, 'F X Velarde Obituary', *The Builder*, 200.6138 (6 January 1961), 22–3; RIBA Journal, 68.7 (May 1961), 264.

2 Raphael Velarde and Francis Xavier Velarde, 'Modern Church Architecture and Some of its Problems', *Clergy Review*, 38.9 (September 1953), 513–26 (p. 526).

3 Derek Bridgwater to Jerzy Faczynski, 24 January 1972, VEL/5/3/1, University of Liverpool Libraries.

4 Notes to log book (diary), May 1945, VEL/3/1/2, University of Liverpool Libraries.

5 Notes by Jerzy Faczynski, 12 March 1972, transcribed by Janet Gnosspelius, VEL/3/3/5, University of Liverpool Libraries.

6 F X Velarde, n.d. 'The Purpose of Criticism', unpublished, VEL/3/2/6, University of Liverpool Libraries.

7 Notes to log book, 9 May 1945.

8 Velarde and Velarde, 513.

9 ibid, 524.

1 Velarde's life and career

1 Julio Ricardo Pastor Velarde, born 1864 in Santiago, Chile, research by Giles Velarde into his family background, 2017.

2 Information from Madge Velarde, interviewed by Jerzy Faczynski and transcribed by Janet Gnosspelius,

12 March 1972, VEL/3/3/5, University of Liverpool Libraries.

3 Memories of Anthony Julian Velarde, 16 February 2004, VEL 4/2/10, University of Liverpool Libraries.

4 *Architects' Journal*, 116.3017 (25 December 1952), 769.

5 F X Velarde Service Record, R/3287, National Archives, ADM 339/1/39327, accessed 16 January 2020; information from Madge Velarde, 12 March 1972.

6 Herbert Thearle, 'F X Velarde Appreciation', RIBA Journal, 68.7 (May 1961), 264.

7 Velarde's deposition made in 1933 as part of an insurance claim following his car accident in 1932, VEL/3/2/7, University of Liverpool Libraries.

8 Often noted as having received a Kitchener Scholarship, there is no record of this and it was more likely a local award.

9 Lionel Budden, *The Book of the Liverpool School of Architecture* (Liverpool: Liverpool University Press and London: Hodder and Stoughton, 1932), pp. 52–4.

10 Thearle, 264.

11 Velarde's log book, 28 May 1945, VEL/3/1/2, University of Liverpool Libraries.

12 Letter from Charles Reilly to Hubert de Cronin Hastings, 9 December 1938, D207/3/8, University of Liverpool Libraries.

13 Thearle, 264.

14 Comment from Giles Velarde, annotated to Velarde's degree certificate, VEL/1/2/3, University of Liverpool Libraries.

15 Information from Madge Velarde, 12 March 1972.

16 ibid.

17 Notes by Janet Gnosspelius, 12 March 1972, VEL/3/3/5, University of Liverpool Libraries.

18 Information from Giles Velarde, VEL/5/1/3, University of Liverpool Libraries.

19 Reported by Giles Velarde, n.d., VEL/3/2/8, University of Liverpool Libraries.

20 Note by Giles Velarde, n.d., VEL/4/2/21, University of Liverpool Libraries. Alcock himself married a great-niece of Cardinal Manning and went on to a successful career with the Office of Public Works in Ireland.

21 'Memories by AJV' (Antony Julian Velarde), 16 February 2004, VEL/4/2/10, University of Liverpool Libraries.

22 Architects' Journal.

23 Testimonies from Francis Xavier and Madge Velarde when making an insurance claim following their accident, late 1933, VEL/3/2/7, University of Liverpool Libraries.

24 'A New Church in Blackburn', review of St Gabriel's by Edward Maufe, Architectural Review, 73 (June 1933), 229.

25 ibid, 229–30. Giles Velarde recounts that Miller and Velarde each produced a scheme, VEL/3/3/5, University of Liverpool Libraries.

26 Manchester Guardian, 19 April 1933, p. 7.

27 Notes by Janet Gnosspelius.

28 Charles Reilly, Architectural Review, 77.460.

29 Nikolaus Pevsner, The Buildings of England, South Lancashire (Harmondsworth: Penguin, 1969), p. 93.

30 'Memories by AJV'.

31 Charles Reilly, 'Note', Art Notes, 1.5 (January–February 1938), 34.

32 Interview with Giles Velarde (DW and AC), June 2014.

33 Velarde's log book, 1 May 1945, VEL/3/1/2, University of Liverpool Libraries.

34 Report of 'The Church and the Artist', conference held 15–18 September 1944, Chichester Cathedral, VEL/4/1/2, University of Liverpool Libraries.

35 Raphael Velarde and F X Velarde, 'Modern Church Architecture and Some of its Problems', Clergy Review, 38.9 (September 1953), 513–26 (pp. 515–16).

36 As recounted by Joy Hockey, a student at Liverpool in the 1940s, to DW, 2016.

37 Notes by Jerzy Faczynski, transcribed by Janet Gnosspelius, 1972.

38 Velarde's log book, 22 October 1945, VEL/3/1/4, University of Liverpool Libraries.

39 Velarde's log book, January 1946–March 1948, VEL/3/1/5, Special Collections and Archives, University of Liverpool.

40 Janet Gnosspelius obituary, Guardian, 10 October 2010, <https://www.theguardian.com/theguardian/2010/oct/10/janet-gnosspelius-obituary> [accessed 6 January 2020].

41 Interview with Giles Velarde.

42 Charlotte Wilman, Urban Redevelopment and Modernity in Liverpool and Manchester, 1918–39 (London: Bloomsbury Academic, 2016), pp. 167–9.

43 *Liverpool Post*, 1 April 1938, cutting held at VEL/4/1/1, University of Liverpool Libraries.

44 Velarde's log book, 28 May 1945. The cathedral authorities agreed to appoint Adrian Scott on 30 May.

45 Velarde's log book entries for January 1945 onwards, VEL/3/1/1, University of Liverpool Libraries; Our Lady of Pity, Greasby, 'Taking Stock: Catholic Churches of England and Wales' <https://taking-stock.org.uk/building/greasby-our-lady-of-pity/> [accessed 19 January 2020].

46 John Owen, 'The Most Rev. John Murphy', *Independent*, 22 November 1995, <https://www.independent.co.uk/news/people/obituary-the-most-rev-john-murphy-1583131.html> [accessed 24 January 2020].

47 Recounted to DW by Anne Saul at St Cuthbert by the Forest, Mouldsworth, 2014.

48 Interview with Giles Velarde.

49 Note from Janet Gnosspelius to Jerzy Faczynski, 9 January 1972, VEL/5/3/1, University of Liverpool Libraries.

50 Velarde and Velarde, 515–16.

51 Notes by Janet Gnosspelius, 11 January 1970, revised 20 February 1972, VEL/5/3/1, University of Liverpool Libraries.

52 Historic Chapels Trust, 'Shrine of Our Lady of Lourdes', n.d., <https://www.hct.org.uk/sites/hct.org.uk/files/inline-files/Shrine%20of%20Our%20Lady%20of%20Lourdes.pdf> [accessed 9 January 2020].

53 *Catholic Herald*, 17 January 1958, cutting in VEL/4/2/1, University of Liverpool Libraries; Interview with Giles Velarde.

54 ibid, p. 247.

55 Velarde commented in his log book for 19 July 1945 that the mason working on the new font for RC St Thomas of Canterbury, Waterloo, Liverpool, was not up to the standard of Tyson Smith, VEL/3/1/3, University of Liverpool Libraries.

56 Velarde's log book, 13 and 28 July 1945, VEL/3/1/4, University of Liverpool Libraries.

57 Thearle, 264.

58 Letter from Janet Gnosspelius to Jerzy Faczynski, 17 March 1972, VEL/5/3/1, University of Liverpool Libraries. Other representatives included Fritz Metzger of Switzerland and Julien de Ridder from Brussels, architects who used innovative methods of concrete construction.

59 F X Velarde, March 1958 diary, VEL/3/2/4, University of Liverpool Libraries.

60 Letter from Janet Gnosspelius to Jerzy Faczynski.

61 Fr Wilfrid Trotman, *Catholic Herald*, 17 January 1958; quoted in St Luke's, Pinner, 'Taking Stock: Catholic Churches of England and Wales' <https://taking-stock.org.uk/building/pinner-st-luke/> [accessed 13 January 2020].

62 Robert Proctor, *Building the Modern Church, Roman Catholic Church Architecture in Britain 1955 to 1975* (Farnham: Ashgate, 2014), pp. 57–8.

63 Dominic Wilkinson, *A New Cathedral, 1960, Designs from the Architectural Competition for Liverpool Metropolitan Cathedral* (Liverpool: Liverpool John Moores University, 2017), pp. 50–1.

64 Herbert Thearle, 'Review of the Shortlisted Entries for Liverpool Metropolitan Cathedral', *The Builder*, 199.6120 (2 September 1960), pp. 413–29.

2 European influences and the 'other modern'

1 Charles Reilly, *Scaffolding in the Sky* (London: Routledge, 1938), p. 127; Peter Richmond, *Marketing Modernisms, The Architecture and Influence of Charles Reilly* (Liverpool: Liverpool University Press, 2001), p. 96.

2 Gavin Stamp, 'Hanseatic Visions: Brick Architecture in Northern Europe in the Early Twentieth Century', lecture to the Twentieth Century Society, 14 February 2008 <http://c20society.org.uk/publica-tions/lectures/gavin-stamp/> [accessed 25 December 2019].

3 Robert Proctor, *Building the Modern Church* (Farnham: Ashgate, 2014), p. 19.

4 Charles H Reilly, *Some Architectural Problems of Today* (London: Hodder & Stoughton, 1924), p. 39.

5 F X Velarde, 'Modern Church Architecture', unpublished lecture, undated, VEL/4/1/1, Special Collections and Archives, University of Liverpool.

6 ibid.

7 ibid.

8 Edward Maufe, *Modern Church Architecture* (London: Incorporated Church Building Society, 1948), p. 51.

9 Jeremy Aynsley, 'Pressa Cologne, 1928: Exhibition and Publication Design in the Weimar Period', *Design Issues*, 10.3 (Autumn 1994), 52–76.

10 *Das Berliner Tageblatt*, 26 May 1928, translated and quoted in ibid, 70.

11 Nikolaus Pevsner, *The Buildings of England: South Lancashire* (Harmondsworth: Penguin, 1969), p. 93, and later revisions.

12 ibid.

13 *Architecture*, 6.32 (May–June 1928), 128–9.

14 Joan Morris ('JUM') 'Churches of Professor A Bosslet', *Art Notes*, 2.4 (March–April 1939), 51.

15 Robert Maxwell recalling his time as a student at Liverpool University School of architecture, personal communication with DW, January 2016.

16 Letter from Giles Gilbert Scott to Charles Reilly, 30 August 1933, Reilly papers D207/40/121, Liverpool University Special Collections and Archives.

17 Personal communication from Giles Velarde to AC, July 2018.

18 ibid. Faczynski confessed to being drawn by the 'magic' of London and the need to look after his parents, newly arrived in Britain. He regretted that when he returned to Liverpool in 1960 it was too late to renew his association with Velarde.

19 Colin Rowe taught at Liverpool between 1950 and 1952, his most famous pupil, James Stirling, being only six years his junior.

20 Destruction witnessed by Desmond Fleet, piano dealer, personal communi-cation to AC, 2014.

21 Petr Pelcak and Ivan Wahla, *Ernst Wiesner* (Brno: Obecní dům Brno, 2005).

22 R Gabriel Pivarnik, *Toward a Trinitarian Theology of Liturgical Participation* (Collegeville, MN: Liturgical Press, 2012), p. 6.

23 Dom Beauduin, *La Piété de l'Église, Principes et Faits* (Louvain: Maredsous, 1914).

24 Romano Guardini, *The Spirit of the Liturgy*, English edition (New York: Sheed & Ward, 1935).

25 Interview with Giles Velarde, DW and AC, June 2014.

26 Proctor, 142.

27 Raphael Velarde and Francis Xavier Velarde, 'Modern Church Architecture and Some of its Problems', *Clergy Review*, 38.9 (September 1953), 513–26 (p. 519).

28 Rudolf Schwarz, *The Church Incarnate: The Sacred Function of Christian Architecture* (Chicago: Regnery Press, 1958).

29 ibid, pp. 39–40, quoted in Kathleen James-Chakraborty, *German Architecture for a Mass Audience* (London: Routledge, 2000), p. 10.

30 Velarde and Velarde, 513–26.

3 Churches of the 1920s and 1930s

1 John Brodie was an engineer of great originality, whose achievements included the invention of goal nets for football in 1889, a prefabricated reinforced concrete cottage of some sophistication and the first Mersey Tunnel. The ring road was constructed as a dual carriageway with generous grass verges, and a central reservation carried a tram track, lined with trees and hedges.

2 Matthew Whitfield, 'Lancelot Keay and Liverpool's Multi-Storey Housing of the 1930s', in *Housing the Twentieth Century Nation*, ed. by E Harwood and A Powers, Twentieth Century Architecture, 9 (2008), pp. 39–50.

3 St Matthew's, Clubmoor, 'Taking Stock: Catholic Churches of England and Wales' <https://taking-stock.org.uk/building/clubmoor-st-matthew/> [accessed 30 December 2019].

4 Letter, 16 July 1923, archive file no. 136, Liverpool Archdiocesan Archives.

5 Biographical notes taken from Mrs Madge Velarde by Janet Gnosspelius 1972, VEL/3/2/5, Special Collections and Archives, University of Liverpool.

6 Letter from Derek Bridgwater to Jerzy Faczynski, 24 January 1972, VEL/5/1/3, University of Liverpool Libraries.

7 Nikolaus Pevsner, *The Buildings of England, South Lancashire* (Harmondsworth: Penguin, 1969), p. 216.

8 Raphael Velarde and Francis Xavier Velarde, 'Modern Church Architecture and Some of its Problems', *Clergy Review*, 38.9 (September 1953), 513–26 (p. 516).

9 Note from Janet Gnosspelius to Jerzy Faczynski, 9 January 1972, VEL/5/1/3, University of Liverpool Libraries.

10 Velarde and Velarde, 520.

11 Interview with Giles Velarde, June 2014 (DW and AC).

12 Lionel Budden, *The Book of the Liverpool School of Architecture* (Liverpool: Liverpool University Press and London: Hodder and Stoughton, 1932), plate 65.

13 ibid, 45; 'A New Church in Blackburn', review of St Gabriel's by Edward Maufe, *Architectural Review*, 73 (June 1933), 229–30; notes by Janet Gnosspelius and Giles Velarde, VEL/3/3/5, University of Liverpool Libraries.

14 *Manchester Guardian*, 19 April 1933, p. 7; *Architectural Review*, 229.

15 Velarde and Velarde, 523.

16 *Manchester Guardian*.

17 *Building*, 9.2 (February 1934), 62–3.

18 J P Alcock, 'Some Contemporary Church and School Buildings of F X Velarde', *Art Notes*, 1.5 (January/February 1938), 35–9.

19 'A New Church in Blackburn'; review of St Gabriel's by Charles Reilly, *Architectural Review*, 77 (April 1935), 163–5.

20 Gavin Stamp, 'Concrete, Brick and Chrome, New British Churches Between the Wars', *Country Life*, 169.4354 (29 January 1981), 238–40.

21 Pevsner, 93.

22 *The Builder*, 200.6138 (6 January 1961), 22–3; RIBA *Journal*, 68.7 (May 1961), 264.

23 Letter from Father Cain to Knowsley Estate Office, 1922, archive file no. 137, Liverpool Archdiocesan Archives.

24 Minutes of Archdiocese Building Committee, 1934, archive file no. 137, Liverpool Archdiocesan Archives.

25 Correspondence December 1934, FDC/53/2/A/22, Liverpool Archdiocesan Archives.

26 *Building*, 12.2 (February 1937), 52–5.

27 Velarde and Velarde, 516–17.

28 Charles Reilly, 'A New Lancashire Church', *Manchester Guardian*, 28 November 1936, pp. 10–11.

29 'Two Modern Churches', *Architect and Building News*, 149 (15 January 1937), 71–5; *Architectural Review*, 81 (January 1937), 23–4.

30 Letter from F X Velarde to Fr Curry at the Archdiocese, 26 December 1934, FDC/53/2/A/22, Liverpool Archdiocesan Archives.

31 *The Builder*, 152.4902 (15 January 1937), 177.

32 Note from Janet Gnosspelius to Jerzy Faczynski.

33 Alcock, 35–9.

34 Interview with Giles Velarde, June 2017 (DW and AC).

35 *The Builder*, 177.

36 *Architect and Building News*.

4 Schools and housing

1 Between 1914 and 1927 the number of pupils in secondary education rose by 60,000 to 367,000. Board of Education pamphlet 50, 1927, quoted in Malcolm Seaborne and Roy Lowe, *The English School, Its Architecture and Organization*, vol. 11, *1870–1970* (London: Routledge & Kegan Paul, 1977), p. 123.

2 In 1929, Percy Jackson, chairman of the West Riding Education Committee, argued that the churches had stood in the way of educational advancement for over a century. Brian Simon, *The Politics of Educational Reform, 1920–1940* (London: Lawrence & Wishart, 1974), p. 174.

3 *Architectural Review*, 80.476 (July 1936), 29.

4 ibid.

5 Susan Poole, 'A Critical Account of the Work of Herbert Tyson Smith, Sculptor and Designer' (PhD thesis, University of Liverpool, 1994), p. 244.

6 The 1936 Education Act proposed to implement the new school leaving age on 1 September 1939.

7 Derek Gillard, 'Education in England, The History of our Schools', <http://www.educationengland.org.uk/> [accessed 22 January 2020].

8 Our Lady of Lourdes and St Joseph's, parish history on line <https://www.birkdalecatholics.com/history/OLOL3.php> [accessed 22 January 2020].

9 *Architectural Review*, 95.568 (April 1944), 91–3.

10 Pevsner did not distinguish the phases of the two buildings. Nikolaus Pevsner, *The Buildings of England, North Lancashire* (Harmondsworth: Penguin, 1969), pp. 235–6.

11 RIBA Journal, 43.18 (8 August 1936), 959.

12 Architects' Journal, 89 (18 May 1939), 811–12.

13 ibid; Architectural Design and Construction, 12.11 (November 1942), 232–3; Architects' Journal, 96 (1 October 1942), 217–22.

14 Log book entry 23 October 1947, VEL/3/1/5, University of Liverpool Libraries.

15 The Baines Committee in 1925 recommended building more cheaply by reducing corridors, halls and roof pitches. Elain Harwood, England's Schools: History, Architecture and Adaptation (Swindon: English Heritage, 2010), p. 64.

16 Log book entry 3 October 1945, VEL/3/1/4, University of Liverpool Libraries.

17 Visits were recorded in Velarde's log book for 1946–8, VEL/3/1/5, University of Liverpool Libraries.

18 The 1944 Education Act finally implemented the raising of the school leaving age to 15 in 1948.

19 Charles Reilly, 'The Body of the Town', Roscoe Lecture delivered at the Royal Institution, 12 March 1934, quoted in Charles Reilly, Scaffolding in the Sky (London: Routledge, 1938), appendix 1, p. 321; Charles Reilly 'The Suburbs We Should Build', Manchester Guardian, 14 February 1941, p. 4; Royal Academy Planning Committee, London Replanned, interim report (London: Country Life, 1942).

20 Reilly based his numbers on ideas developed by Lewis Mumford about the ideal size for a community. Charles Reilly papers, D207/25/4, University of Liverpool Libraries.

21 Thomas Sharp, Town and Countryside (Oxford: Oxford University Press, 1932); Thomas Sharp, English Panorama (London: Architectural Press, 1936).

22 'Birkenhead: Community versus Segregation', Architects' Journal, 100.2584 (3 August 1944), 86, quoted in Peter J Larkham, 'New Suburbs and Post-War Reconstruction, The Fate of Charles Reilly's "Greens"', Working Paper no. 89, School of Planning and Housing, University of Central England (2004), p. 57.

23 Notes by Janet Gnosspelius, 11 January 1970, revised 20 February 1972, VEL/5/3/1, University of Liverpool Libraries.

24 Log book entry 5 March 1947, VEL/3/1/5, University of Liverpool Libraries.

5 Post-war churches

1 Velarde (Val) to Charles Reilly (Prof), 15 October 1947, D207/4/4, Special Collections and Archives, University of Liverpool.

2 The Builder, 172.5438 (9 May 1947), 440, 444.

3 CHC 10/174, Liverpool Archdiocesan Archives; Jerzy Faczynski biographic notes dictated to Janet Gnosspelius, 1972, VEL/3/2/5, Special Collections and Archives, University of Liverpool; St Aidan's, Huyton, Towards the Future (Liverpool: privately printed, 1992).

4 Report on St Aloysius, Roby, archive file no. 161, Liverpool Archdiocesan Archives.

5 St Aloysius, Roby, 'Taking Stock: Catholic Churches of England and Wales' <https://taking-stock.org.uk/building/roby-st-aloysius/> [accessed 7 January 2020].

6 Our Lady of Pity, Greasby, 'Taking Stock: Catholic Churches of England and Wales' <https://taking-stock.org.uk/building/greasby-our-lady-of-pity/> [accessed 7 January 2020].

7 Notes, for example 22 January 1945, log book, VEL 3/1/1, Special Collections and Archives, University of Liverpool.

8 Our Lady of Pity, Greasby.

9 Interview with Giles Velarde, August 2018 (DW).

10 Nikolaus Pevsner and Edward Hubbard, *The Buildings of England, Cheshire* (Harmondsworth: Penguin Books, 1971), p. 370. Revised by Clare Hartwell and Matthew Hyde, Yale University Press, 2011, p.153.

11 National Heritage List for England, no. 1390589, amended 18 September 2013.

12 St Cuthbert by the Forest, Mouldsworth, 'Taking Stock: Catholic Churches of England and Wales' <https://taking-stock.org.uk/building/mouldsworth-st-cuthbert-by-the-forest/> [accessed 8 January 2020].

13 Bill Cresswell, *A History of St Cuthbert by the Forest, Mouldsworth, 1955–2005* (Tarvin: privately published, 2009), pp. 16–18.

14 John Tarn, personal notes on a list of Velarde churches, prepared for a lecture to the Dean and Chapter of Liverpool Metropolitan Cathedral, date unknown.

15 St Theresa's, Upholland, 'Taking Stock: Catholic Churches of England and Wales' <https://taking-stock.org.uk/building/upholland-st-theresa/> [accessed 8 January 2020].

16 Raphael Velarde and Francis Xavier Velarde, 'Modern Church Architecture and Some of its Problems', *Clergy Review*, 38.9 (September 1953), 513–26 (pp. 522–3).

17 *Bootle Times*, 24 June 1955, p. 1.

18 *Bootle Times*, 2 August 1957, p. 1; cutting in VEL/4/1/12, University of Liverpool Libraries.

19 Historic Chapels Trust n.d. 'Shrine of Our Lady of Lourdes' <https://www.hct.org.uk/sites/hct.org.uk/files/inline-files/Shrine%20of%20Our%20Lady%20of%20Lourdes.pdf> [accessed 9 January 2020].

20 Interview with Robin Riley (DW).

21 Historic Chapels Trust n.d.; interview with Giles Velarde, June 2014 (DW and AC).

22 Interview with Robin Riley.

23 *The Builder*, 200.6138 (6 January 1961), 22–3; interview with Giles Velarde, June 2014.

24 Holy Cross parish records, Diocese of Shrewsbury Archives; *Catholic Building Review*, northern edition (1959), 117–19.

25 Pevsner and Hubbard, p. 95.

26 *Wirral News*, 5 July 2006, p. 3; Holy Cross, Bidston, 'Taking Stock: Catholic Churches of England and Wales' <https://taking-stock.org.uk/building/birkenhead-holy-cross/> [accessed 27 January 2020].

6 The London churches

1 Interview with Giles Velarde, August 2018 (DW).

2 Robert Proctor, *Building the Modern Church, Roman Catholic Church Architecture in Britain 1955 to 1975* (Farnham: Ashgate, 2014), p. 57.

3 Note from Janet Gnosspelius to Jerzy Faczynski, 9 January 1972, VEL/5/3/1, University of Liverpool Libraries.

4 Daniel Lysons, 'Harrow-on-the-Hill', *Environs of London*, vol. 2, *County of Middlesex, London* (1795), pp. 559–88

<https://www.british-history.ac.uk/london-environs/vol2/pp559-588> [accessed 13 January 2020].

5 Giles Velarde, VEL/4/2/4, University of Liverpool Libraries.

6 Joyce Kemp, *The Spiritual Path of Caryll Houselander* (London: Paulist Press, 2001), p. 78.

7 *The Builder*, 109.3798 (19 November 1915), 366.

8 Bernard A Harrison, *St Luke's Catholic Church, Pinner, The Story of a Parish* (Pinner: Mark/Lucy Enterprises, 2007).

9 St Luke, Pinner, 'Taking Stock: Catholic Churches of England and Wales' <https://taking-stock.org.uk/building/pinner-st-luke/> [accessed 21 January 2020].

10 Note from Janet Gnosspelius to Jerzy Faczynski, 20 February 1972, VEL/5/3/1, University of Liverpool Libraries.

11 Note from Janet Gnosspelius to Jerzy Faczynski, 9 January 1972.

12 Preliminary drawings dated 13 July 1959, AAW/DOW/PAR/14, Westminster Diocesan Archives.

13 ibid.

14 ibid.

15 Note by Giles Velarde, n.d., VEL/5/1/3, University of Liverpool Libraries.

16 Brochure, *St Edmund of Canterbury Catholic Church, Whitton*, 1934–2009, VEL/4/2/15, University of Liverpool Libraries.

17 Letter from Julian Velarde to William Holford, January 1961, D147/LA19, University of Liverpool Libraries.

7 Velarde's legacy

1 J P Alcock, 'Some Contemporary Church and School Buildings of F. X. Velarde', *Art Notes*, 15 (January/February 1938), 39.

2 Personal recollection of DW as a masters' student at Liverpool University School of Architecture during the late 1980s.

3 Interview with Giles Velarde, June 2014 (DW and AC).

4 Herbert Thearle, 'F X Velarde Appreciation', RIBA *Journal*, 68.7 (May 1961), 264.

5 Gavin Stamp, 'Hanseatic Visions: Brick Architecture in Northern Europe in the Early Twentieth Century', lecture to the Twentieth Century Society, 14 February 2008 <http://c20society.org.uk/publications/lectures/gavin-stamp/> [accessed 25 December 2019].

6 In 1944 Velarde drew up a list of all his friends, living and dead, from all aspects of his life. VEL/3/2/1, University of Liverpool Libraries.

List of works

Triptych detail St Teresa's, Upholland

Velarde drawing of first scheme for proposed church of Our Lady of Lourdes, Hillside, Birkdale

1930–1936
Our Lady of Lourdes RC Primary School
Grantham Road, Southport, Merseyside PR8 4LT
Client: RC Diocese of Liverpool
Designed by F X Velarde
Architectural Review, 80.476 (July 1936), 29
Architects' Journal, 84 (23 July 1936), 116–17
The temporary chapel was demolished when the new parish church opened in 1956

1931
Guildford Cathedral★★★
Competition organised by Diocese of Guildford
Unplaced entry by F X Velarde

1932–1933
St Gabriel's Anglican church★
Brownhill Drive, Blackburn, Lancashire BB1 9BA
Client: Diocese of Blackburn
Designed by F X Velarde, notionally assisted by Bernard Miller
Substantial alterations involving removal of parapets and addition of metal cladding
Architectural Review, 73 (May 1933), 229–30
Building, 9.2 (February 1934), 62–3
Nikolaus Pevsner, *The Buildings of England, South Lancashire* (Harmondsworth: Penguin, 1969), p. 93
Fiona Ward, 'Merseyside Churches in a Modern Idiom', in *The Twentieth Century Church*, Twentieth Century Architecture, 3 (1998), pp. 95–102

1933–1936
St Monica's RC church
Fernhill Road, Bootle, Merseyside
L20 9GA
Client: RC Diocese of Liverpool
Designed by F X Velarde
Listed at grade II in 1981, upgraded
to grade I in 2017
Charles Reilly, 'A New Lancashire Church',
Manchester Guardian, 28 November 1936,
pp. 10–11
Architect and Building News, 149 (15 January
1937), 71–5
Architects' Journal, 85 (7 January 1937), 12–13
The Builder, 152.4902 (15 January 1937),
169–70, 177

RIBA Journal, 49 (23 January 1937), 272
Architectural Review, 81 (January 1937), 23–4
Building, 12.2 (February 1937), 52–5
Nikolaus Pevsner, *The Buildings of England,
South Lancashire* (Harmondsworth: Penguin,
1969), p. 93

1934
Bexhill on Sea pavilion
competition★★★
Organised by Bexhill Corporation
Unplaced entry by F X Velarde

1934
Building Trades Exhibition Stand★★
Liverpool

Green Shutters, house for Mr and Mrs Curran, Bourne End, Buckinghamshire

Client: Accrington Brick & Tile
Company
Designed by F X Velarde
Architects' Journal (3 October 1935)

1936
Luton Secondary School for Boys
competition★★★
Organised by Luton Education
Committee
Unplaced entry by F X Velarde

1937–1942
**Our Lady of Lourdes RC Secondary
School**
Grantham Road, Southport,
Merseyside PR8 4LT
Client: RC Diocese of Liverpool
Designed by F X Velarde
Architectural Review, 95.568 (April 1944), 91–3

1938
St Monica's RC junior boys' school★★
Aintree Road, Bootle, Liverpool,
Merseyside L20 9EB
Client: RC Diocese of Liverpool
Designed by F X Velarde
Art Notes, 1.5 (January–February 1938)
Catholic Herald, 15 January 1937

1938–1939
House in Oswaldkirk, Yorkshire, for
Mr and Mrs Blackden, cost £900
Mr Blackden taught at Ampleforth

1939–1942
Scalby Senior School★
Fieldstead Crescent, Scarborough,
North Yorkshire YO12 6TH
Client: North Riding County
Council, Frank Barraclough director
of education

Designed by F X Velarde
Architects' Journal, 89 (18 May 1939), 811–12
Architectural Design and Construction, 12.11
(November 1942), 232–3
Architects' Journal, 96 (1 October 1942), 217–22

1939–1952
(initial designs were delayed due to
WW2, built 1949–52)
St Aloysius RC church
Twig Lane, Roby, Liverpool,
Merseyside L36 2LF
Client: Fr M J O'Sullivan,
Archdiocese of Liverpool
Designed by F X Velarde

1940
Our Lady and St Benedict's RC
church★★★
East End, Ampleforth, North
Yorkshire YO62 4DA
Client: Fr Aelred Graham, RC
Diocese of Middlesbrough
Designed by F X Velarde, unexecuted
Art Notes, 4.3 (Summer 1940), 28–9

1945–1946
St Joseph's, Crosby
Altar rails, made by Tyson Smith,
and stained-glass window
F X Velarde log book, 12 March 1945,
VEL/3/3/1, University of Liverpool Libraries

1945–1946
St Thomas of Canterbury, Waterloo,
Crosby
Pulpit
F X Velarde log book, 19 July 1945,
VEL/3/1/3, University of Liverpool Libraries

Velarde's unrealised design for Our Lady and St Benedict RC church, Ampleforth, North Yorkshire

1945–1947
St Alphonsus RC church, alterations;
new primary school and boys' club★★
Stanley Road, Bootle, Merseyside
Client: RC Diocese of Liverpool
Designed by F X Velarde, assisted by
Gerald Beech

1945–1952
(built 1951–2)
Our Lady of Pity RC church★
Mill Lane, Greasby, Wirral,
Merseyside CH49 3NN

Client: RC Diocese of Shrewsbury
Designed by F X Velarde, assisted by
John Prescot
External buttresses added in 1950s
designed by Velarde to counter
spreading of external walls
A new presbytery was added in 1974
designed by Richard O'Mahony
Architects' Journal, 116.3017 (25 December
1952), 769
Nikolaus Pevsner and Edward Hubbard,
The Buildings of England, Cheshire
(Harmondsworth: Penguin, 1971), p. 226

Altar and triptych, Christ the King RC church, Bromborough, Wirral, carved by Herbert Tyson Smith for Velarde's brother Father Raphael Velarde

1945–1957
Christ the King, Bromborough
High Altar, and Lady Chapel in
church hall building
Client: Raphael Velarde
Catholic Building Review, northern edition
(1958), 76

1946
Masterplan competition for new
Federal University of Oye★★★
Oye, Nigeria
Shortlisted entry by F X Velarde

1946–1947
Our Lady of Sion convent
alterations★★
Acton Burnell Hall, Shrewsbury,
Shropshire SY5 7PF
Client: Sisters of the Order of Sion
Designed by F X Velarde, assisted by
Janet Gnosspelius
Alterations to the chapel, dining
hall and accommodation block all
now remodelled as part of Concord
College

1946–1947
Hall Green housing estate★★★
Salop Street, Bilston, West Midlands
Client: Bilston Borough Council
Designed by F X Velarde and
G G Dobson to a pattern established
by Charles Reilly

1946–1949
Our Lady of the Rosary RC church★★
and presbytery★
Winifred's Drive, Donnington,
Telford, Shropshire TF2 8BA
Client: RC Diocese of Shrewsbury
Designed by F X Velarde, assisted by
John Prescot

1947
Colombo Cathedral★★★
Competition organised by The Royal
Society of Arts
Second place by F X Velarde
Journal of the Royal Society of Arts, 95.4742
(9 May 1947), 377–9
The Builder, 172.5438 (9 May 1947), 440–5

1947–1949
Our Lady of Compassion RC church
(interior fittings only)★
School Lane, Formby, Merseyside
L37 3LN
Client: RC Diocese of Liverpool
Interior fittings designed by
F X Velarde altering a 19th-century
church by Henry Clutton

1947–1949
St Mary's College science and
teaching blocks
St Mary's College, Everest Road,
Crosby, Liverpool, Merseyside L23
5TW
Client: The Christian Brothers
Designed by F X Velarde, assisted by
Janet Gnosspelius

1947–1951
Holy Cross RC primary school*
Gaultby Road, Bidston, Birkenhead,
Merseyside CH41 7DU
Client: Fr Burke and Fr Rigby, RC
Diocese of Shrewsbury
Designed by F X Velarde

1948–1949
St Aidan's RC church**
Adswood Road, Huyton, Liverpool,
Merseyside
Client: Archdiocese of Liverpool,
Fr Thomas Maher
Designed by F X Velarde incorpo-
rating an RAF hangar

1948 onwards
St Bede's Secondary School
Chester

1949–1954
(built in two phases 1954–8 and
1959–60)
St Aidan's RC infant and junior
schools*
Adswood Road, Huyton, Liverpool,
Merseyside L36 7XR
Client: Lancashire County Council
Designed by F X Velarde and Jan P de
Waal
The infant school was remodelled as
a new church 1990–2
Catholic Building Review, northern edition
(1956), 160

1949–1955
St Columba's RC primary and
secondary schools**
Hillside Road, Huyton, Liverpool,
Merseyside L36 8BL
Client: Lancashire County Council
Designed by F X Velarde and Jan P de
Waal
Architects' Journal, 110.2840 (14 July 1949), 33

1950–1953
English Martyrs RC church
St George's Road, Wallasey, Wirral,
Merseyside CH45 6TU
Client: RC Diocese of Shrewsbury
Designed by F X Velarde
Listed grade II in 2003, upgraded to
grade II* in 2013
Nikolaus Pevsner and Edward Hubbard,
The Buildings of England, Cheshire
(Harmondsworth: Penguin, 1971), p. 370

1950–1957
(built 1955–7)
**Thanksgiving Shrine of Our Lady of
Lourdes**
Whinney Heys Road, Blackpool,
Lancashire FY3 8NU
Client: RC Diocese of Lancaster
Designed by F X Velarde
Listed grade II* in 1999

1952
Ursuline RC primary school (hall
only)*
Nicholas Road, Blundellsands,
Liverpool, Merseyside L23 6TF
Client: RC Diocese of Liverpool
Designed by F X Velarde and Jan P de
Waal

1952–1957
(built 1955–7)
St Teresa RC church
College Road, Upholland,
Skelmersdale, Lancashire WN8 0PY
Client: RC Diocese of Liverpool
Designed by F X Velarde
Listed grade II in 1999

c 1952–59 (built 1956–9)
St Thomas More RC Secondary
School★★
Scot Lane, Newton-le-Willows,
Wigan, Lancashire WN5 0UA
Client: Lancashire County Council
Designed by F X Velarde, assisted by
Janet Gnosspelius and K C Duncan
Demolished early 2000s

1953–1954
St Anselm of Canterbury RC
church★★
Thirlmere Road, Chorley, Lancashire
PR7 2FY
Client: RC Diocese of Liverpool
Designed by F X Velarde

1953–1955
St Cuthbert by the Forest RC church
Station Road, Mouldsworth,
Cheshire CH3 8AL
Client: RC Diocese of Shrewsbury
Designed by F X Velarde
Listed grade II in 2014
Nikolaus Pevsner and Edward Hubbard,
The Buildings of England, Cheshire
(Harmondsworth: Penguin, 1971), p. 284
B Cresswell, *A History of St Cuthbert by the
Forest* (Tarvin: privately published, 2005),
p. 16

Nave, St Gabriel's RC church, Alsager

1954
St Benedict RC church (Lady Chapel only)
Market Street, Hindley, Wigan, Lancashire WN2 3AA
Client: RC Diocese of Liverpool
Lady Chapel and internal fittings designed by F X Velarde altering 19th-century church by Joseph Hansom

1955
St Gabriel's RC church★
Lawton Road, Alsager, Cheshire ST7 2DE
Client: RC Diocese of Shrewsbury
Designed by F X Velarde
Nikolaus Pevsner and Edward Hubbard, *The Buildings of England, Cheshire* (Harmondsworth: Penguin, 1971), p. 59

1955
St Mary Magdalene RC church★★
Forester Avenue, Much Wenlock, Shropshire TF13 6EU
Client: RC Diocese of Shrewsbury
Designed by F X Velarde

1955–1956
St Michael and All Angels RC primary school
New Hey Road, Woodchurch, Birkenhead, Merseyside CH49 5LE
Client: RC Diocese of Shrewsbury/ Birkenhead Borough Council
Designed by F X Velarde and Jan P de Vaal

1955–1957
St Alexander's RC church★★
St Johns Road, Bootle, Liverpool, Merseyside L20 8BH
Client: RC Diocese of Liverpool
Designed by F X Velarde
Catholic Building Review, northern edition (1957), 45; (1958), 54–5

1955–1959
Holy Cross RC church
Hoylake Road, Bidston, Birkenhead, Merseyside CH41 7BU
Client: RC Diocese of Shrewsbury
Designed by F X Velarde
Listed at grade II in 2003
Nikolaus Pevsner and Edward Hubbard, *The Buildings of England, Cheshire* (Harmondsworth: Penguin, 1971), p. 95
Catholic Building Review, northern edition (1959), 117–19

1956
St Winefride's RC church
Crowmere Road, Shrewsbury, Shropshire SY2 5LA
Client: RC Diocese of Shrewsbury
Designed by F X Velarde
Listed at grade II in 2014

1956–1958
Basilica of St Pius X
Boulevard Remi Sempe, 65100, Lourdes, France
Client: RC Diocese of Tarbe and Lourdes
Designed by Pierre Vago with an international consultative committee including F X Velarde as the UK representative

Elevation study for ss Vincent De Paul and Louise Demarillac RC church, Potters Bar, Hertfordshire

1957
The Grail (chapel only)
Waxwell farmhouse, Waxwell Lane, Pinner, London HA5 3EP
Client: The Grail Society
Designed by F X Velarde, assisted by Janet Gnosspelius

1957–1958
St Luke's RC church
Love Lane, Pinner, London HA5 3EX
Client: RC Diocese of Westminster
Designed by F X Velarde, assisted by Janet Gnosspelius
Listed at grade II in 2016

1957–1962
(built 1960–2)
ss Vincent De Paul and Louise
Demarillac RC church★★
Mutton Lane, Potters Bar,
Hertfordshire EN6 2AT
Client: RC Diocese of Westminster
Designed by F X Velarde and
completed after his death by
F X Velarde Partnership

1958
St Mary and St John's church★
Crow Lane, Newton-le-Willows
Triptych (now removed)
Richard Pollard and Nikolaus
Pevsner, *The Buildings of England,
Liverpool and the South-West* (London:
Yale University Press, 2006), p. 526

Our Lady of Pity RC church, Harlescott, Shrewsbury

1959
Study for adaptions to St Phillip Neri
RC church★★★
Catherine Street, Liverpool,
Merseyside L8 7NL
Client: RC Diocese of Liverpool
Designs by F X Velarde unexecuted,
project undertaken by Weightman &
Bullen

1959–1960
Liverpool Metropolitan Cathedral★★★
Competition organised by RC
Diocese of Liverpool
Unplaced entry by F X Velarde

1959–1961
Our Lady of Pity RC church
Meadow Farm Drive, Harlescott,
Shrewsbury, Shropshire SY1 4PU
Client: RC Diocese of Shrewsbury
Designed by F X Velarde and
completed after his death by Richard
O'Mahony of the F X Velarde
Partnership

1959–1962
**St Teresa of the Child Jesus RC
church**
Shenley Road, Borehamwood,
Hertfordshire WD6 1TG
Client: RC Diocese of Westminster
Designed by F X Velarde and
completed after his death by Richard
O'Mahony and Janet Gnosspelius
of the F X Velarde Partnership with
assistance from Giles Velarde

1960–1963
St Edmund of Canterbury RC church
St Edmund's Lane, Nelson Road,
Whitton, Middlesex TW2 7BB
Client: RC Diocese of Westminster
Designed by F X Velarde and
completed after his death by Richard
O'Mahony of the F X Velarde
Partnership

1960–1965
St Michael and All Angels RC church
New Hey Road, Woodchurch,
Birkenhead CH49 5LE
Client: RC Diocese of Shrewsbury
Initial designs by F X Velarde; a
different scheme was realised after
his death by Richard O'Mahony of
the F X Velarde Partnership
Listed at grade II in 2014
Architecture North West, 114 (December 1965),
6–7
Architects' Journal, 143.15 (13 April 1966),
941–52
Wood, 32.5 (May 1967), 32–3
Nikolaus Pevsner and Edward Hubbard,
The Buildings of England, Cheshire
(Harmondsworth: Penguin, 1971), p. 106

Further reading

Published texts by Velarde

Raphael Velarde and Francis Xavier Velarde, 'Modern Church Architecture and Some of its Problems', *Clergy Review*, 38.9 (September 1953), 513–26

Secondary Works

100 Churches, 100 Years, ed. by Susannah Charlton, Elain Harwood and Clare Price (London: Batsford, 2019)

Bill Cresswell, *A History of St Cuthbert by the Forest, Mouldsworth, 1955–2005* (Tarvin, privately published, 2009)

Andrew Crompton and Dominic Wilkinson, 'F X Velarde, an English Expressionist', *Journal of Architecture*, 24.3 (May 2019), 325–39

Bernard A Harrison, *St Luke's Catholic Church, Pinner, The Story of a Parish* (Pinner: Mark/Lucy Enterprises, 2007)

Elain Harwood, 'Neurath, Riley and Bilston, Pasmore and Peterlee' in *Housing the Twentieth Century Nation*, ed. by E Harwood and A Powers, Twentieth Century Architecture, 9 (2008), pp. 83–95

Elain Harwood, *England's Schools: History, Architecture and Adaptation* (Swindon: English Heritage, 2010)

Kathleen James-Chakraborty, *German Architecture for a Mass Audience* (London: Routledge, 2000)

Nikolaus Pevsner, *The Buildings of England, North Lancashire* (Harmondsworth: Penguin, 1969), revised by Clare Hartwell (New Haven, CT and London: Yale University Press, 2009)

Nikolaus Pevsner, *The Buildings of England, South Lancashire* (Harmondsworth: Penguin, 1969), revised in two volumes by Clare Hartwell (New Haven, CT and London: Yale University Press, 2004) and Richard Pollard (New Haven, CT and London: Yale University Press, 2006)

Nikolaus Pevsner and Edward Hubbard, *The Buildings of England, Cheshire* (Harmondsworth: Penguin, 1971), revised by Clare Hartwell and Matthew Hyde (New Haven, CT and London: Yale University Press, 2011)

Susan Poole, 'A Critical Account of the Work of Herbert Tyson Smith, Sculptor and Designer' (PhD thesis, University of Liverpool, 1994)

Robert Proctor, *Building the Modern Church, Roman Catholic Church Architecture in Britain 1955 to 1975* (Farnham: Ashgate, 2014)

Peter Richmond, *Marketing Modernisms, The Architecture and Influence of Charles Reilly* (Liverpool: Liverpool University Press, 2001)

Joseph Sharples, *Charles Reilly and the Liverpool School of Architecture 1904–1933* (Liverpool: Liverpool University Press, 1996)

Gavin Stamp, 'Hanseatic Visions: Brick Architecture in Northern Europe in the Early Twentieth Century', lecture to the Twentieth Century Society, 14 February 2008 <http://c20society.org.uk/publications/lectures/gavin-stamp/>

Matthew Usher, 'The Churches of F X Velarde' (MArch dissertation, Liverpool John Moores University, 2017)

Fiona Ward, 'Merseyside Churches in a Modern Idiom: Francis Xavier Velarde and Bernard Miller' in *The Twentieth Century Church*, Twentieth Century Architecture, 3 (1998), pp. 93–101

Dominic Wilkinson, *A New Cathedral, 1960, Designs from the Architectural Competition for Liverpool Metropolitan Cathedral* (Liverpool: Liverpool John Moores University, 2017)

The Twentieth Century Society

Without the Twentieth Century Society an entire chapter of Britain's recent history was to have been lost. It was alert when others slept. It is still crucial!
SIMON JENKINS, WRITER, HISTORIAN, JOURNALIST

The Twentieth Century Society campaigns for the preservation of architecture and design in Britain from 1914 onwards and is a membership organisation which you are warmly invited to join and support.

The architecture of the twentieth century has shaped our world and must be part of our future; it includes bold, controversial, and often experimental buildings that range from the playful Deco of seaside villas to the Brutalist concrete of London's Hayward Gallery. The Twentieth Century Society produces many publications of its own to increase knowledge and understanding of this exciting range of work. The Twentieth Century Architects series has enabled the Society to extend its reach through partnership, initially with RIBA Publishing and now with Historic England, contributing the contacts and expertise needed to create enjoyable and accessible introductions to the work of architects who deserve more attention. In the process, the books contribute to the work of protecting buildings from demolition or disfigurement.

We propose buildings for listing, advise on restoration and help to find new uses for buildings threatened with demolition. Join the Twentieth Century Society and not only will you help to protect these modern treasures, you will also gain an unrivalled insight, through our magazine, journal and events programme, into the ground-breaking architecture and design that helped to shape the century.

For further details and to join online, see www.c20society.org.uk

CATHERINE CROFT
DIRECTOR

Other titles in the series

Ahrends, Burton and Koralek
Kenneth Powell
Apr 2012
978-1-85946-166-2

Aldington, Craig and Collinge
Alan Powers
Nov 2009 (out of print)
978-1-85946-302-4

Alison and Peter Smithson
Mark Crinson
Jun 2018
978-1-84802-352-9

Arup Associates
Kenneth Powell
Jun 2018
978-1-84802-367-3

Stephen Dykes Bower
Anthony Symondson
Dec 2011
978-1-85946-398-7

Chamberlin, Powell & Bon
Elain Harwood
Nov 2011
978-1-85694-397-0

Wells Coates
Elizabeth Darling
Jul 2012
978-1-85946-437-3

Frederick Gibberd
Christine Hui Lan Manley
Sep 2017
978-1-84802-273-7

Howell Killick Partridge & Amis
Geraint Franklin
Jun 2017
978-1-84802-275-1

McMorran & Whitby
Edward Denison
Oct 2009
978-1-85946-320-8

John Madin
Alan Clawley
Mar 2011
978-1-85946-367-3

Robert Maguire & Keith Murray
Gerald Adler
Mar 2012
978-1-85946-165-5

Leonard Manasseh & Partners
Timothy Brittain-Catlin
Dec 2010
978-1-85946-368-0

Powell & Moya
Kenneth Powell
Apr 2009
978-1-85946-303-1

Ryder and Yates
Rutter Caroll
Apr 2009
978-1-85946-266-9

Forthcoming titles

Architects' Co-Partnership
Alan Powers
978-1-84802-575-2

Edward Cullinan
Kenneth Powell
978-1-84802-557-8

Ralph Erskine
Elain Harwood
978-1-84802-559-2

Ernö Goldfinger
Elain Harwood and Alan Powers
978-1-84802-274-4

Patrick Gwynne
Neil Bingham
978-1-84802-276-8

Peter Moro
Alistair Fair
978-1-84802-561-5

John Outram
Geraint Franklin
978-1-84802-558-5

Walter Segal
John McKean
978-1-84802-560-8

William Whitfield
Roland Jeffery
978-1-84802-573-8

Peter Womersley
Neil Jackson
[ISBN tbc]

Illustration credits

The author and publisher have made every effort to contact copyright holders and will be happy to correct, in subsequent editions, any errors or omissions that are brought to their attention.

Andrew Crompton
p 36, p 61, p 66, p 138, p 150

Bristol University Archive
p 109

Deutsches Architekturmuseum
p 37, p 38

Dominic Wilkinson
p 43, p 120, p 121

Elain Harwood
p 42

Historic England
(Photographer James O Davies) p x (DP031027), p 4 (DP031019), p 99 (DP180683), p 106 (DP031028), p 107 (DP031023), p 108 (DP031020), p 120 (FF003634)

(Photographer Chris Redgrave) p 4 (DP264556), p 28 (DP264563), p 37 (DP264748), p 122, p 124 (DP264740), p 125 (DP264741), p 128 (DP264538), p 129 (DP264546), p 130 (DP264620), p 131 (DP264746), p 132 (DP264553), p 133 (DP264560), p 135 (DP264564)

(Photographer Alun Bull) Foreword (DP234563), Front cover (DP233956), Frontispiece (DP234565), p 3 (DP234526), p 16 (DP234529), p 25 (DP233950), p 45 (DP234531), p 48 (DP234537), p 52 (DP234577), p 54 (DP234578), p 55 (DP234580), p 64 (DP234524), p 71 (DP234528), p 72 (DP234530), p 91 (DP234574), p 92 (DP234576), p 94 (DP234538), p 97 (DP234543), p 98 (DP234557), p 100 (DP234572), p 102 (DP234614), p 103 (DP234617), p 111 (DP233971), p 114 (DP233951), p 115 (DP233961), p 136 (DP180682)

(Photographer Steven Baker) p 88 (DP235132), p 104 (DP235138), p 105 (DP235162), p 138 (DP235123), p 159 (DP235121), p 162 (DP235152)

Liverpool Diocesan Archives
p 40

Matthew Usher
p 67, p 118, p 119

National Trust
p 6 (150127), p 15 (149609), p 36 (149627), p 65 (149605), p 70 (149613), p 59 (149844), p 60 (149843), p 111 (149615), Back cover

RIBA Drawings and Archives
p 80, p 81 (RIBA71934), p 82 (RIBA71937), p 83 (RIBA31040), p 139 (RIBA11314)

Robin Riley
p 113

Shrewsbury Diocesan Archives
p 117

University of Liverpool Libraries
p 8, p 10 (Reilly papers), p 11, p 12, p 13, p 16, p 17, p 18, p 20, p 23, p 26, p 28, p 30, p 34, p 51 (149628), p 53, p 58 (149622), p 68, p 74, p 76, p 77, p 78, p 79, p 85 (Reilly papers), p 86 (Reilly papers), p 95, p 106, p 112, p 126, p 134, p 152, p 153, p 155, p 156, p 161

Virtual Museum of Nurenberg
p 40 (Theo Noll)

Index